DEDICATION

Dad, you were there in the beginning, making sure I knew that there were other options available. You were there in the middle when I scurried back to corporate safety, But you always made sure I had what I needed to be a success in that business called "My Own"

Paul Zamarra was the first person I ever met, who deliberately gave up a multi million dollar career in order to teach. He taught me some business a lot of drafting, but mostly he aught me to have the confidence to stand up and speak what was on my mind.

Michele has made every morning a joy and coming home every night a sanctuary. Thanks for your love and support.

CONTENTS

Jerome L. Hess

FORWARD

So far, our journey has taken us from getting hired into the perfect job that we have always dreamed of, through the levels of growth needed for management. Our intrepid hero has recovered physically, mentally and now wants to take that most emotionally frightening of choices, that of starting ones own business.

Whether you choose to run a Mexican Taco and Holistic Fish Stand from an old Airstream trailer, or want to lay the foundation for a Multi Billion Dollar Real Estate Empire, there are certain skills that you can acquire that will help you navigate the booby traps that seem to be waiting for everyone strong enough to stand up and yell "Mine!"

Walk with us and learn from the lessons that have been experienced both personally and through observation. After all if experience is the best teacher than surely someone else's experience is the most economical education available. Not to mention that every danger you can sidestep may be as much as a year off of your learning curve.

As you take this journey you may find yourself saying "I've been there" or "That sounds like..." Rest assured that all the events and people are real, the names and circumstances have been interchanged to protect the innocent.

Jerome L. Hess

1. So you THINK you want to be an Entrepreneur?

Let's look a little closer, just to be sure.

The dictionary defines it this way*: one who organizes, manages, and assumes the risks of a business or* ENTERPRISE Which is a fair definition of the word. But as one who has actually performed in this role, I would have to suggest that the term encompasses a *whole* lot more! So let's actually begin with what **you** think the term means, and I will compare that with experience and see how close we are.

Referencing a 2009 Online poll of 1800 Business men and women, when asked what the word "Entrepreneur" means the most popular answer was: **Small Business Owner.**

How does Small Business Owner fit with Entrepreneur? Well to start with an Entrepreneur could be anyone who generates an income based solely on their own merits from an enterprise of their own design. So from that description one of America's largest Entrepreneurs would be Bill Gates. After all he owns what was at one time, a "small business", he just figured out, in short order, how to grow and develop that business into a rather large one. However in the same vein couldn't the man in the Ice cream Truck also be an Entrepreneur? Although I personally have never owned an Ice Cream Truck, I do have a very good business partner who owned one for several years and just like Bill Gates, he figured out, rather quickly, how to turn his into a, for him, very large business, pulling in a net in the very high 5 figures.

Now if you're Bill Gates, or even a worker in IT you may laugh at the idea of the man selling push ups to your 5 year old could be considered an Entrepreneur. Certainly it would take an Ice Cream vendor of great self image to place himself in the same conversation as Bill Gates. Even his High 5 figure income compared with the Ten's of Billions of dollars difference that Mr. Gates earns, spans a substantial gap. But when you consider the origin of both you start to see more similarities than differences. Bill Gates started his company in his garage; Joe the Ice Cream Man didn't have a garage so instead it was a picnic table under an Oak Tree. They both started very small, with a very basic product selection, in Gates arena, he really only started with DOS. Joe started with the Ice Cream treats that he could buy from his local warehouse. Now some folks would point to that and say there is your primary differentiator, that Joe bought his products from someone else, and therefore instead of an entrepreneur he was instead a Re-Marketer. Well if you look though your computer history books you'll find that Bill gates didn't write Dos, he bought it from someone else. The *primary* difference, and perhaps the reason that Bill is a multi billionaire, and Joe wasn't, is that Bill went on to negotiate an exclusive distribution deal with the largest supplier of computers at the time. That would have been akin to Joe negotiating to become the "Official Dessert" of the US Army. But it didn't work out that way.

So, small business owner, that is indeed one component of being an Entrepreneur, but is it the **only** component? Do you have to be a reseller of things to be an entrepreneur? Well maybe, after all people will always want to buy **things**! But if that were the prime qualifier it would leave out one of my all time favorite Entrepreneurs. Chuck spent 25 years in the US Navy, retiring finally to become a full time real estate developer. Within 2 years of his retirement he owned several Real Estate companies an insurance company and a few development corporations. Additionally he was a real estate investor, buying and selling homes, land and subdivisions for profits. I thought $800 a month retirement pay was good, the incomes he developed in just a few short years were of a size that my mind couldn't even grasp. Surely he would be considered an Entrepreneur, but he didn't own a "small" business, nor did he make anything. Instead, he found a hole in an industry and plugged it, by providing unsurpassed customer service, and treating everyone as though they were a million dollar client, he not only had customers, but *repeat* customers that referred him business. That's not only the **best** kind of business, but it's also the easiest sale!

Finally I ask you to peak at Phil, Phil is what we call a "serial Entrepreneur", when he was just leaving high school he worked with an older man who put up fences for a living. Although the man knew a great deal about placing and measuring and putting up a fence on a tight schedule, he knew almost nothing about business. Phil hadn't taken any business courses in school, but he could watch what his boss was doing, and not doing, and quickly figure out which one made the most money. So in short order he started his own fence company. As in many of these stories Phil's former employer actually worked for Phil at one point, finding it easier to be an employee than a boss. For years Phil did everything he could to promote and grow his fence business, including incorporating things that he saw other business owners doing, who were **not** in the fence business. After a decade Phil was able to very tightly control not only his employees, his income and his schedule, but was actually able to niche himself in a very tight segment of the fence business. That of designing custom gates and operators, and actually turn away, what most companies considered their "bread and butter."

Knowing that the fence business was not the peak of his achievement he started another business, a business that although diametrically opposed (or so it seemed) to the fence business, it was a business that could teach him many great business principles. He learned skill with people, proper accounting practices, delayed gratification, all these things, while building a very successful "side business." Although his initial plan was, I believe to make his 'side business' his primary business he found a new dream.

Phil had 4 children, all of them in school at about the same time, all of them very athletic. What he discovered was that there were not enough folks willing to volunteer to coach the children's sports teams, and then on the rare occasions where there were enough people, they were lacking in many basic items, like transportation. So Phil started volunteering, this of course drew some of his attention from his other businesses, but his new dream started to develop more and more. What he was dreaming of was a way to become the coach, the mentor and the transportation for these teams of kids, so that they would always have at least one consistent factor in their lives. For some of these children Phil was the *only* stable factor in their lives.

As his 'side business' grew, he started developing good solid relationships with many people, the likes of which he never could have hoped to reach. In doing so he found that there were some very wealthy people in his area who had some very nice motor coaches, motor coaches that sat unused the majority of the time. Even when empty they still required care and feeding. Phil's idea was that if he could gather enough people together like this, he could drive their coaches, during their downtimes, this would provide great transportation for the kids, keep the Motor Coaches in use, as well as give him exposure he needed to people whose business it was to buy and sell vehicles like this.

A few years later he bought his own coach, then another, and another and another. During the week he, or one of his drivers, would drive a coach to a wedding or football game or concert, and on the weekends, they could use the coaches as team transportation for the kids. Thus allowing him to be a constant and stable influence in his kid's lives, and making sure that when they are traveling, they are doing so in a safe and healthy manner. So Phil takes the term Entrepreneur and tweaks it one level more, a serial Entrepreneur is someone who goes from one business to the next, all owned by him, all giving him the freedom to do what he needs to do. Most of all he gets to earn a living and have a life all at the same time.

What you have seen so far are a few examples of some folks who have built their businesses from the ground up and made very large successes, what I haven't exposed you to yet, is what they went through **during** the trip from zero to hero, or what their failures felt like. You will be exposed to both of these as we go, as well as a great deal more as we make our way through to becoming the "Remote Control Entrepreneur." But for right now I want to ask a few questions that I don't expect you to answer immediately, but to think about during our journey together.

For example, will you be starting from scratch or will you be franchising or buying an existing business? They all have their ups and downs, the main reason you may decide to start from the ground up is the lower perceived initial investment. After all, if you, like Joe, decided that you wanted to sell person to person, you would need to "rent/buy" a vehicle large enough for storage that would be equipped sufficiently to keep your products from melting. Whereas if you were going to buy an existing business, or buy into a franchise, your initial entry fees might be quite a bit more than you ever imagined, but it would be more of a 'turn key' operation.

If you wanted to buy a free standing ice cream shop, you could, if you had sufficient capital, purchase the entire business at the beginning, take on partners to help spread the financial responsibilities around, or you might approach the current owner about *him* financing the purchase. Understand that in preparing a business for sale, most business owners will be advised to set their selling price anywhere between 2 years and 10 years Gross Income. So if the Ice Cream shop your looking at brings in any kind of "living wage" say between $40,000 and $100,000, your purchase price could fall between $80,000 and $1 Million dollars.

Let's say instead you wanted to purchase a franchise, the best part about these is that traditionally they come with a "system" that is almost 100% foolproof. This system contains all accounting, and vendor information, and comes through a "university" that consists of a series of classes that are mandatory for their owners, thus everyone starts off on the same foot. Of course the shoe for this foot typically will *start* at an investment of between $100,000 and over $1million dollars depending on the host companies reputation and whether the franchise includes a real estate purchase or not.

The nice part about deciding to buy a franchise is that once you make the decision the hard part is over right? Of course with that decision will come the nights where you are praying that you will meet the payroll, or that the vendor who has owed you for six months will suddenly have a change of heart and deliver your products on schedule. Then of course there was always knowing where the main breaker box is so that on those rare occasions where a "bank error" not in our favor, would result in a rather dark establishment. See, although the 'difficult decision' ends once you decide to buy a franchise, it will be followed by thousands of smaller decisions each and every day.

Please don't let me lead you to believe that business is all sweat and worry. However I do want to make sure that as President Truman made famous, when you **own** the company, large or small "The Buck Stops Here." Meaning that when your name is on the sign outside that says "Owner, Franchisee or Captain of His Fate" you are the last and first person that people come to when there is an issue. So be prepared.

Do any of these situations sound attractive to you? If you don't see yourself in these situations, you don't have to; it's just easier within the confines of this book. But do you see yourself in any part of any or all of these folks? Do you have a dream? Not just to own a business, but one that will survive the tough times? Do you have the desire to be the one person that has the final answer on everything? Are you willing to become the person that you need to, who will be able to not only stand up for your company and your employees, but for your customers as well? Seeking to find equitable solutions no matter who is at fault?

More importantly, are you ready, willing and able to *learn*? College does a great job of teaching you how to get a job; they do a crummy job of teaching you how to own a business. So for the next 200+ pages we're going to do everything we can to generate the tips, the tools and the ideas that you will need to become the proud owner of that business called **YOUR OWN.**

2.   Starting Out Small.

If we had to start at the beginning, we would find ourselves hunched over a two wheeled bicycle during the summer of my 5th grade school year. That was where my very **first** business started and stopped. As my dad took our entire days gross, all $19.27 of it, and subtracted the raw materials I had gotten from mom's kitchen. Sugar, Kool-Aid, cups. Then the cost of the wood I used to construct the lemonade stand, plus it seemed as though every kid in the neighborhood convinced my dad that they were "independent contractors" who were out canvassing the streets in the name of advertising for me (honest I don't remember saying it to more than 2 or 3 kids), and leaving my partner and I with an entire days *net* income of 17 cents – **between us**.

Some folks probably would have called that a failure, but you know I can walk down the mall here locally and point out a ½ a dozen stores that would probably be open today if they had only made a profit of 17 cents a day. But in most retail scenarios its usually not as straight forward as that. For now, lets jump ahead a few years to my junior year in High School, Mom and Dad had bought a house right downtown in our city, three blocks off the main drag. But more importantly this was a turn of the last century home that had a detached "carriage house" that a previous owner had turned into a fully functioning and independent dwelling. It could have been large enough to rent out as an efficiency, but instead my parents allowed me to turn it into a photo studio. At the time I was the head photographer of the school newspaper and yearbook, as well as regularly published in the city and county paper, so this would finally allow me to do some studio work with portraits and still life's and the like. Additionally I was just starting to get involved with film and lighting for commercials, this was before home video.

For three months dad and I worked on installing a fully functioning lab, and placing the lights we would need as well as the multi colored backdrops and stands to hold them all. When I finally opened for business there were only 2 studios in town that were not located in a SEARS. One of them was about 4 blocks from me, and the other was on "the other side of the tracks." So I thought I had it made, and for the first few months so did dad, I did groups families, wedding parties, you name it I was working it. Then as fate would have it I was on assignment from one of the local papers to cover a "horse auction", and ran into a small "slick gentleman" in the shiniest suit I had ever seen, he rapidly asked if I was a photographer, I handed him a business card and said yes, and he offered me a job on the spot.

As it turned out I had just been tapped by the **largest** magazine publisher focused on the Equestrian Lifestyle in the United States. He wasn't looking for an employee as much as an independent contractor to cover the parties and auctions and what not, whenever these types of events were in town. Back then this was fairly often, had I the same fiscal responsibility that I try and exhibit today, I can firmly say that I could have attended all four years of the college of my choice, and not had to worry about a dime!

If I had been more fiscally responsible. See even though I generated more income during the 1 or 2 weeks a quarter when he was in town, than I did working as a part time graphic artist, I would still find myself broke at the end of every month. I was working a part time job, in addition to my photography, and my photography paid 7 to 8 times as much, in the same period of time, yet it all went in one account and out the next. At that point in my life, anyone could see I had the attitude for an Entrepreneur, just not the business skills. So I did what most of Middle America does when faced by that kind of an issue. I went to school!

Although I spent a great deal of time in college, that's not the school I went to, instead I looked around for Entrepreneurs and small business owners willing to teach me, and sat at their feet and asked every and any question I thought they would answer. Of course in my house, with my dad there, I didn't have to go very far, but I also knew the value in getting answers to questions from several different sources. So although dad lay a great foundation in my life, when I had a question that didn't seem to be in his domain or when he specifically directed me to look elsewhere that's exactly what I did. You would be amazed at just how talkative folks can be! After all, ask anyone, their favorite subject, the one they will gladly spend the most time talking about, is themselves.

The 'part time job' that I had after school and on weekends, wasn't with the local hamburger chain. I had found the largest privately owned company of its kind, in our town, and made myself useful there. Frequently working 4 to 6 hours every day after school and then another 10 to 12 every Saturday and Sunday.

My best friends father was a 'Serial Entrepreneur' who had gone from dolphin trainer, to business owner in one step then preceded to build a business to a profit point and then sell it, roughly every 5 years. Even the professors in school that I studied with, the ones that I spent the most time with and the ones I learned the most from, taught as a sidebar, having a very large and profitable corporation on one side, and playing in one of the only swing bands to make a profit on the other. In every case I would work quietly and diligently to prove I was serious about learning what they wanted to teach me, instead of just "studying for the test."

From these instructors I learned many things that were not placed in the texts that we were required to read. Instead there was almost always a secondary, optional reading list. With instructors such as Dale Carnegie, Zig Ziglar or Ben Franklin. These 'texts' were there to open my mind to the way of thinking in a broader sense. I began to find that people were more than just employees filling a role; these were people very much like me, some of who would one day progress to the point where they too would want to be their own boss. Additionally were the lessons that required me to think about how to work with those folks who didn't want **anything** else. Although they seemed almost alien to me at the time, the idea of working in one job, for 20, 30 or even 40 years until retirement came one day, was absolutely frightening..

It did take some time, but I did come to understand that those folks are needed. We all need someone who wants to come in every day, day after day, and do their job, then go home. This was never made clearer than when a "joke" started coming true. During one of my stints working for someone else I made it a very strict policy that my team was to use every effort available to teach another team that we had to work with on a regular basis, how to perform certain tasks. So, my team, being good at what they did, taught certain members of this other team some of our tricks of the trade.

Their respective managers were so impressed by their "initiative", that they would promote our 'trainees' right out from underneath us! After about the 5th person that this happened to we suddenly had the majority of that team clamoring to know what we taught. On one hand it created a new "type" of work for my team, that of training. However it also took us out of what we should have been doing and into a situation where we became very valued as trainers.

From my experience there are several very valid reasons to start small, however with every good comes some bad, so let me lay out a few options for you, to demonstrate both sides of the coin, where I can, and let you make your own decision.

If your goal is to start your own business, regardless of the type (sole proprietor, franchise etc.) starting small has one very big advantage; the book keeping is very easy. Chances are good that you will have a small selection (possibly one) of products or services, with a restricted pricing schedule, and potentially fixed costs.

So on a regular basis you will have X products being sold at Y cost subtracting Z fixed expenses. Everything after Z is yours. Now this is the perfect time to learn about proper accounting, the first 10% in your pocket the next 10% to charity the next 10% to savings and the remaining 70% reinvested in your business.

That's one way to view a small business or sole proprietorship, on the off chance that your thinking is a bit larger than that, much of what you learn in a small business will directly translate to a large one, with some caveats:

1)   **Partners** – you don't need them, and unless you're married to them you don't want them. Notice I didn't say dating them. I can not tell you how many great businesses I have seen torn apart because a couple who weren't married, started a business, and one of them made a mistake or got tired of waiting. I used to be more liberal on this policy but I see it happen time and time and time again. The only time you will change that is when there is a clear and total understanding in writing of the 50/50 nature of the business including how things will be resolved in the case of a dissolution.

2)   Office Space – again, you don't need it, until you need it. One of the hardest things I have to teach my 5 year old is the vast difference between want and need. I know you want a nice plush office, I know you want to see your name on the door, and I know how cool it is to have a secretary. I also know that each and every one of those things costs money, and lots of it. There are folks who will not understand that your supplier was late, or you had more returns than allocated, etc. In the electronic world we live in, unless you are a heart surgeon, you don't need an office for quite some time, and chances are even they don't start with an office.

3)   NEW Computers, cars ,furniture etc. – I will be the first one to tell you that you do need some type of computer, and a printer would help as well. Unless your business is going to be Graphic Arts or Sound/Video editing you do not need cutting edge technology. You do not need a color printer, you do not need new furniture, to furnish the office you don't need. You most especially do not need new vehicles.

I had a very good friend of mine whose fiancée determined that he needed more variety in his personal life. To get back at him she decided she would become a successful business owner. I thought she had a great idea, as did her father, who leveraged his retirement fund to get her started. Against my advice they bought 2 new commercial vans, new computers, and new Cell phones, new clothing to act as uniforms and printed literature by the thousands.

The one thing she forgot was to canvas her target market to see if *they* thought it was a great idea. Unfortunately after a year, which is typically the minimum time to test a new idea, all her money was gone, she determined that she had the right business at the wrong time. I know that she filed bankruptcy, it was a rather personal and very sensitive matter so I didn't ask how dad was doing, but I can not imagine it helped his retirement much. Bottom line is, for $30 you can get a brand new no frills pay as you go cell phone from 7 – 11, every pawn shop in the world has decent PC's from $200, and a good laser printer is $100 new. Everything else should have been bought as needed. Cost of entry would have been a fraction of what she invested, when your lean you can make very fast course corrections as you need them.

4)   SOLE is not ALONE – We will cover all of these subjects in greater detail elsewhere, but if you don't have a mentor that has experience in the core of your business, then you need to find one. Or Two! I'm not talking about Great Aunt Martha who made millions with the pet rock. I'm not bashing the pet rock; I am questioning just how much business experience she has in what you want to do. If the pet rock is her only experience, and you want to establish a door to door dry cleaning valet, then go find someone who has done, if not that, then some part of that. Maybe they have owned or even managed a Dry Cleaning store, or owned a delivery service, or something that would qualify them as having some good sound advice that they could offer.

Trust me you will not be lacking for advice, you will however need a very large and capable filter in order to discern that which is valid and that which is white noise. For some reason folks want either to be part of your success, or to have been the first to have warned you of impending doom when things go in one of two directions, as they will. Seek out at least one, perhaps up to 10 mentors whom you can open up and be accountable with. Someone who knows if you're not telling the truth and someone whom you will feel bad about disappointing. Seek out and create a mastermind group of these people.

Finally, understand this, everything, absolutely everything started as an idea, a spark, maybe even a dream in someone's mind. Someone has had that thought, maybe even you, and that thought is now being turned into a reality. Each and every large business or corporation, and its concepts started as a small thought, a thought that someone wanted to try, and someone else believed in. Once established and moving in a positive direction, then you may plan world domination. But lets conqueror our own little corner of town first.

More importantly, are you ready, willing and able to learn? College does a great job of teaching you how to get a job; they do a crummy job of teaching you how to own a business. So the rest of this book is dedicated to giving you the tools you need to become the proud and successful owner of that business called: **You're Own.**

3.   Researching your Idea

At one time or another we all have the idea, the one that **you** just know is going to propel you into orbit in a matter of weeks, or months at the latest. How can you discreetly find out if the idea that you have is worthwhile, if its currently being pursued or if its just a few too many taco's before bed time? If you have taken our course of Writing Your Book in 21 Days you will find some of this very familiar, and if you haven't, you should. But I digress, much of the research that you perform in developing a central theme to a new book is going to relate exactly to determining if your business idea has merit.

I will be treating this as though it were a new idea that you had, and not, for example, a franchise or existing business that you are buying, although I would encourage you to perform many of the same search functions to make sure your new business will be supported. In the case of a franchise the "home office" should have performed this for you. However you will want to perform some of them specific to your location, as you may be more familiar with the neighborhood, than a simple set of statistics would show.

So, you have an idea of the type of business you want to open, in a live training event I would ask the attendees to throw out some ideas and the one that sounded like the most "fun" I'd go with, today lets start simple. You are a computer programmer who through layoffs has found herself with more time on her hands than she would like, and **much** less money in the bank than you need, therefore, since jobs are scarce, some kind of business would be ideal.

My first question is, what's your current skill set look like? No don't submit your resume, I'm not hiring and that's not what's going to get you a business anyway! What have you done besides program computers? Did you work in college? Did you have summer jobs? Do you have a friend that owns a business that you have helped with during times of duress? I have a friend of mine who used to volunteer helping out in a Greeting Card shop during High School, when she got to college the manager of the card store now owned her own business and so she worked as a counter person in a shipping store! The skills weren't the connection in that case, the people were, and that often will work out as well!

Alternatively, and this can get into dangerous areas, what do you enjoy doing and what are you good at? There is a saying that runs through business seminars every few years and it will typically go something like this: "When you *love* what you do you'll never work another day in your life!" Wow, that sounds really cool doesn't it? Yeah, I thought so to, until I found that many folks who tried to turn their hobby into a business either get burned out on their hobby or they have a business that no one is interested in. For example just because you like cutting the toenails on Pot bellied pigs, doesn't mean you can own a day spa for Pot Bellied pigs and start pulling down a million dollars a year!

So, what's your idea? Well it just so happens that you have dogs, and you like animals. Interestingly enough you even find some sadistic pleasure in bathing the dog (and your brothers cat) and of course since you want everything just right, you typically will add a bow to the collar or a holiday appropriate bandana. Sounds like were moving towards a pet salon doesn't it? So, now we need to consider what kind? Stationary or Mobile? They both have huge benefits and the start up costs are not much different. The challenge with a stationary business is location, the challenge with mobile is getting the word out.

So lets write down a few of the startup costs of each and see how the balance against each other:

STATIONAIRY: License, Sales Tax, Location, Store Front Rent, Equipment, Advertising, Consumables (soap, conditioners etc) Towels, "freebies" (bandanas etc), Signage, Insurance (property and business), Utilities (Power, Water, Sewage) and more.

MOBILE: License (if you cross city/county borders will you need more than 1?), Sales Tax (is the tax the same everywhere you will go?) , Service Area (how FAR will you go), Vehicle cost (rent, buy/New, used?), Vehicle Equipment, Advertising, Consumables (soap, conditioners etc) Towels, "freebies" (bandanas etc), Signage on vehicle, Insurance (Vehicle and Business), gas and more.

This is in **no way** a comprehensive list, you will want to consult as many resources as you can to get a more detailed list but I think this starts to demonstrate that there are not as many start up differences as one would imagine. In the end, depending on your vehicle cost, do you buy it new or used and your conversion costs; your first 90 days could be the exact same investment. When seeking out research sources I would strongly suggest that you use your local phone book, and book some time (offer to pay) to talk to the owners of each kind of business.

Believe it or not, as long as you're not setting up shop right across the street from them, most business owners will gladly tell you much more than you would ever imagine. If you want to interview a Mobile groomer, look for one in the next town or county over. If your town is big enough, it may be sufficient to just look on the opposite side of town. Most mobile groomers that I know (believe it or not I know 4 of them) have a 30 mile radius; outside of that they don't really care! You will probably also find that the majority of them started on their own, with little or no help. One store owner I know bought a grooming salon and before she built it up enough to justify hiring a full time staff, she would bring in her teen age kids and let them perform the busy work, while she took care of the animals and the register.

Now comes the research that will pay off in double rewards. This is the research that can give you a clear picture of how profitable this may be as well as how you want to design the name. So lets fire up the PC and head on over to Google. In Google you are going to put in as specific and detailed search terms as you can to get close to what YOUR business will be, and look for the results with your notepad. So, you have determined that you want a mobile grooming salon that, naturally, runs off of appointment only! Also you have determined that you ONLY want to serve the Greater Osceola County Area. Go to Google and type in "**mobile pet grooming**", "**Osceola County**" please, note where I have the quotes. Some use quotes some use parenthesis, check the advanced help.

That exact set of terms yields 751 results. Believe it or not although that sounds huge, it is not as large as it seems. 751 results, take a few minutes and scan through the first 10 pages, subtract 2 things right off the bat. First, look at the addresses for the sites (at the bottom of the result) and anytime you see a duplicate listing don't count the duplicate. Next, from their descriptions, look for anything that appears to be information only, normally that's anything with forum in the listing.

Doing so from our first 10 pages we actually result in 20 unique listings for mobile pet groomers that appear to service Osceola County, interestingly enough there is even one listing that is someone looking to sell their mobile grooming business. That is someone you want to talk with! Next look at the last 10 pages, and do the same! Even I was interested when, after looking at the last 10 pages and crossing out everything that was something unrelated, an information only site, or a site from the first 10 pages, I was left with **one** additional listing So, from 751 returns we have 21 unique listings.

Now the hard part is looking through those 21 listings and seeing what your competition actually is. Many of these folks will list their prices (bad idea because folks will compare prices, and web sites don't change as often as the Sunday circular), but it will also give you an impression of the level of success these folks are experiencing. People who are very successful in their businesses, or very active in their businesses will update their web sites often.

Now we move into the area that Google and several other sites, are the champions at, yet they were never intended to be, and that is in the area of helping you name your business. You may think that Bobbie Soxer's Mobile Dog Wash is just the Cat's Meow when it comes to business names, but the fact of the matter is, that may mean nothing to anyone under the age of 30! So lets look at how we can use these free tools that are available, and let them show us how folks are searching for items on the internet! In your 751 returns search for the most common words that you can find, a simple CTRL-F should help. You see on their websites home pages. Now you're going to take your 21 valid web pages and do the exact same thing, except you are looking at their home page (the 1st page you get to when you click their link) and you are looking for the 5 most common words. This sounds like a lot, but the easiest way I have found is to copy the text off the home page (File/Edit/Select All the copy) and paste it into a word document. There you should be able to search the commonalities fairly easy.

Once you have your list of *five* most common words, lets see what kind of name you can come up with them. Lets say that the 5 words are: **PET, DOG, CAT, GROOM, MOBILE.** Those are all very good words, but you are going to want to include one word that describes what will set you apart, it maybe **SERVICE,** or **CARE**, or **TENDERNESS** that's your choice, but think about how you would want your pet treated at a groomers, and the words should come pretty easy. Now you have SIX words, to use in your "word jumble" in search of a name. Maybe something like **Kissimmee Kate's Mobile Grooming with a Heart.** (Kissimmee is the largest city in Osceola County) Or **Groomers on Wheels throughout Osceola.** Maybe even **Pet Groomers who Care Wheeling About Osceola.** You see the idea, use as many of the terms that folks are searching for as you can. Now, once you come up with your name, move to at least two more sites, and start searching. The two I recommend for this are YouTube and Facebook.

Now on Facebook, you're gong to perform a search more like you did on Google; you're looking to see what's out there and if there is enough interest for Generation X to be involved. After you search Facebook you going to move to YouTube. YouTube is one of the 5 fastest growing search sites in

America. It's not just for films that didn't make the cut on Americas Funnies Home videos, On YouTube however you are going to use your prospective name first! See what; if any results you get with just your name, then, much like you did in order to develop your name, you will want to use some small combinations of those words, some of which may not even make any sense. YouTube is just going to look for selected matches. I promise you will find some very strange things and it will not all be G rated, so make sure the kids are in bed. Once you have gone through those websites (and there are plenty more), you should start to focus in on several very important things.

The first should probably include something basic, like "Is this a viable business?" If *no one* is looking for you, or what you have to offer than you are creating a nightmare, and an extreme marketing challenge. I'm not saying that you don't want to pursue it; I am however saying that you may want a backup plan in place! Alternatively it could just mean that you don't yet have a handle on what terms folks are using to search for their mobile grooming service. In which case you should either refine your terms and narrow your search, or broaden your terms and use a wider criteria. Then just try to search again. Now if all of this sounds like hard work, it is. Could you outsource this work and get it done inexpensively? Possibly, but you need to know how the searches were performed so that one day when your outsource leads just dry up, you know how to get more. On the other hand it could be very expensive, if done improperly.

I met an author recently who asked about my cover artwork, when I told him how I got it done and to what cost he almost passed out. He had gone to his local graphic artist (as recommended by his publisher), and he had invested over $3500 in the same amount of artwork (my investment was less than $100). So, yes there are other ways to get this done, but you need to know how to do it, just in case.

So, you have done some preliminary research, you have interviewed a few of the folks who either own or work for people who are doing what you want to do, now what? Well on the one hand I could say, well you've spent about a week, performing your due diligence, go for it and lets get this business on the road! However I couldn't sleep if I sent you out in the world ill prepared, so instead I think that next we will talk about some of the biggest mistakes folks make when they first get started!

Jerome L. Hess

4. 10 Common Mistakes *Most* Entrepreneurs Make...

...During their first few weeks.

1) Too High Expectations - Business

I hate for *this* to be the first thing, but I also don't want anyone deciding that they want to go in business for themselves only to find that their first months outgo exceeded their income by a factor of 10, and be surprised by it. Business, like life, is hard. There is no question about it, and much like life, when managed from the proper perspective, business can become one of the 3 most rewarding things you do. Family and Worship taking the other 2 spots.

Unfortunately all too often, a new business owner thinks they're going to make millions in their first few years. This rarely happens in most businesses, and unrealistic expectations can kill your business. Not to mention what it will do to your relationships, your attitude and the feelings of those folks around you. The best thing you can do is to set realistic goals and **time frames** to achieve them, *then* do everything you have to do to make them happen. You notice I bolded Time Frame, we haven't started to talk about that but there is a very simple way to set yourself up for success on your timetable. Take this next section for example:

I am sitting on a business right now where someone 30 years earlier was able to earn $100,000 part time in their first year. More recently, folks entering into this industry have found themselves earning as much as $60,000 per month by the end of their first year. So when I map out my expected 'income' for the first year of my new business, which figure do you think I should use?

How about neither. Please do not let me burst anyone's bubble about the income potential of their new "Pot Belly Pig Day Spa." All I am asking you to do is plan it out conservatively, realistically, but conservatively. What's the best way to do that? Why I'm glad you asked.

When you're working on your initial 1st year business plan, start slowly and move from there. Lets take our Mobile Pet Grooming salon for example. After careful study and research you have determined that your total out go in month one will be approximately $35,000. Now look at your second month and see what kind of recurring expenses you can expect, rent, uniforms, gas, supplies etc.

In all your number crunching you have determined that you're recurring average expenses will be $1,200 per month. You have priced yourself so that you average pet groom will be priced at $50; you now know that you need to groom 24 dogs every month just to break even. Break even, that's no money for you. But that's also only 1 animal per day. If you have determined that you can average 10 animals per day, then with a full calendar you should be breaking even by the 1st Wednesday of every month.

How full is your calendar going to be that first month? Or even the first week? Remember earlier when we talked about having 6 months of your expenses in savings? Well in this case you would need to have $7200 in the bank, just so you could meet your expenses every month. If you can do that then your first few weeks, possibly even your first few months, should be A- OK. But you know that you going to have to start turning a profit pretty quickly or the taste of dog hair is going to be unbearable. But you have a plan, so you know that by your third week your calendar is going to be filling up quickly. Can you maintain your expectations for the amount of time it's going to take you to get from 0 to profit for that first month?

2) Not enough cash on hand combined with the inability to get investors.

Now, if you flip back to the cover you will notice that there is nothing there that talks about "success on a shoestring" or any other indicator that I will be talking about having a business with zero investment. I am very big about you not spending too much money on the wrong things, and I hate to see folks invest too much in the wrong areas, but you will need some type of seed program available.

The number of ways to develop a 'seed program' is almost as long as the list of businesses available, however here are a few of the more common ones that you're going to consider. More importantly, please pay attention to the caveats.

a) **Budget** – I know that we haven't discussed this yet (and we may not), but before you open your doors, whether they are virtual or stone, you need to draw up as accurate and realistic of a budget as you possibly can. When you do so, write it as though you are spending the "last dollars that you have in the world", and include everything. Rent, utilities, uniforms, office supplies, advertising, payroll (even if its just you, you're going to need to eat), office equipment. Once you're done, then copy it and forecast it out for no less than 6 months, preferably a year. While you are writing this budget you will also be including as many different sources of income as you possibly can, and be as realistic as you can. If you're in the mortgage business, but you just got your license, do not base your budget on closing a $750,000 loan every month. Especially not in this market. Understand that many businesses have *zero* income for the 1st 30 days (some longer), so if you're un realistic about your income expectations, everything else is probably going to go downhill from there.

b) **Savings** – Again, I don't recommend you using the kids college funds as your startup money, BUT if you have to "borrow" a small (10%) portion to fund an investment that can give you a return of between 3 and 5 times your investment, it's probably a good idea. Use THIS as your guideline when determining what money to use, "Can I afford to lose every penny of this money?" So using ALL of the kids college fund, bad idea, 10%, painful but not life ending. One would hope that you have a properly funded 'rainy day' fund where you have stashed enough $ to cover your bills for 6 months, that would be a bad source of seed money. But if your rainy day fund has enough to cover 12 months, it might be something to think about.

c) Partners – A wise man said once "A silent partner will not remain so for long." Now whether he meant remain silent or remain a partner I don't know, but I have seen both things happen and it is not a pretty sight. So consider any and every partnership on its own individual merits and ask yourself if the business goes south, will your relationship? If the answer is yes, then you probably don't want to use that as a source. I determined long ago that if I wasn't married to a person I wouldn't do business with them, so far this has worked out very well for me. But you have to understand that I have no common sense, my wife has a great deal, and on more occasions than not I actually listen to her!

d) Family – Bad idea. 'Nuff said. No really, it should stop here and now. There are hundreds if not hundreds of thousands of families that have broken up over money; Personally that's the worst idea in the world. There are probably exceptions, but I can't think of any.

e)   Refinance your Home, Car, Boat etc. – I hope
that our entire nation has learned that this is a bad idea.
In our nations History Real Estate has never lost so
much value as it did in 3 short years, in the mid 2000's.
But that doesn't mean it couldn't happen again.

**f)   Government and Private Programs (grants, sba
loans etc)** – Do you have any portion of any minority in
you of any kind? I know a young lady who received at
$10,000 grant to open a cleaning business because she
was 1/32nd Polish. She applied for a Grant from the
Polish American Society of XYZ (her area) and won the
grant. It can take some research, and some time, but I
have another young lady who has secured several
hundred thousand dollars for her kid's educations
through various ethnically central grant programs. The
money is out there, it's up to you to find it.

Now, this is just a small scratch of the surface of the
sources of money, either to get started or to stay running,
but please pay attention to some of the caveats, these will
become very important. The other thing to remember is
don't wait until the last minute. If you even start to think
that you might use an infusion of cash, start investigating
your sources!

3) Trying To Do It All Alone

Everyone wants to be the hero, we all want to be Rocky at the end of the movie (the odd numbered films), and we all want to be able to say "I did it my way and on my terms." Believe it or not history records most of those folks as – losers. Not that there is anything wrong with losing, as long as you learn from the experience and keep moving on!

Many business owners however never consider that they may be in a spot where they need qualified help. This is a very big mistake. Entrepreneurs sometimes find it very difficult to not only accept help when its offered but most find it extremely tough to admit that they need some help. Most will find themselves in a spot where they need to almost surround themselves with a quality team that is dedicated to helping them succeed.

In today's age of electronic media this is actually much easier than it has been in the past. You may log into a forum of like minded business owners, or perhaps just a networking group in the area, this may provide them with the surroundings they need to work through their issue. Often just hearing that someone else in the group has a similar issue could provide them the moment's relaxation they need to actually find the solution!

Even if that isn't possible, lets look to that great tome of wisdom that we all should have read by now "Think and Grow Rich", and understand the miracles that can be performed when you have a key "Master Mind Group" established. Preferably made up of live folks but if need be you may even want to develop a "super squad" as he did, and assemble a group of the greatest folks who can help you in a time of crisis.

4) Poor Customer Service

If you don't get this one, or I have to explain too much, close the book, send it back to me and I will give you a full refund. I don't believe that there is any way that this can be stressed too much. I can't think of a single business that doesn't live and die by it's customer service. I was going to sarcastically say "grave digger" but I would imagine that's one group of folks you really don't want to upset!

Really, good customer service is so easy to perform, especially in a day and age when average has become the acceptable standard. But let me say it like this, "ghost shop" the folks who are in businesses like yours, see how the staff treats you, would you come back? If the answer is yes, ask yourself why. If price is the only answer you can come up with, than that business will not be a competitor for very long.

Along the same vein, have someone (or do it yourself) ghost shop your business, see how the customer service stacks up against your own expectations. Now how it compares to the other guys. They aren't paying you, you compare yourself against your best expectation. If they do not exceed that, then take every step you need to in order to correct that actions. Don't stop until it is right.

5) Unscrupulous Employment Practices

Along the same line as #4, if you are not treating your folks fairly, they will **not** be reciprocating to you or your customers. You may be the only face that your customers ever see, but if you're not treating your suppliers fairly, how long do you think your products are going to be shipped on time and correctly?

Many business owners get caught up in the idea that because they pay people "under the table" that they have certain rights or privileges to do as they please. This is illegal as I am sure you know but there are consequences to doing this. Not only will both you and your employee have to repay the government for taxes that should have been paid; you will also be fined and in some cases, your business will be shut down.

Previously we have talked about protecting your reputation? Well this is one thing that will kill that faster than anything. You may have a whole shelf of "Boss of the Year" awards, but if the media finds one employee who is not being treated the way they should, they will be sure to spread that over every newscast they can, and "your side" of the story will never be heard. Worse yet, most folks won't listen closely to what is being said, they will just see you and or your business being caught up in the news, and that's not a good place to be seen!

6) Failure To Maintain A Website/ Failure to Advertise

Now I have grouped the two of these items together because although they may not be mutually exclusive can you imagine any company not hosting a good website, while trying to "get the word out?" It really doesn't matter what it is that you have chosen to do for your business, in today's market hosting a website can be considered as much a part of advertising as it is a general idea of who you are and what you represent. But for a moment lets look at these independently.

> a. **Failure to Advertise** – This comes about most often because an Entrepreneur has neglected to budget properly for this in their planning and budgeting expenses. Then as they are just getting started they get a visit or phone call from their friendly "Phone Book" sales rep, who explains "all about advertising in the local markets."

> This would be great, if this 'expert' hadn't been selling coupons or newspaper subscriptions the month before. I don't mean to knock what may very well be a great industry, but ask yourself, do you even know where your yellow pages are at this moment? Mine go right in the recycle bin every year when they come out. Why, we get 2 copies for every phone number we have, and that starts to add up. One year I did actually decide to hang on to one of the books, and after I had not used it for over a year, I decided that I was on the right track!

> Which brings me to the other part of advertising, when you do plan for it, remember to include *not* just the media that you may be considering, but also think about the business that you are establishing. If you are

making all hard wood pre assembled Bed Frames that have been sold off the back of a "horse drawn buggy" for the last 200 years, maybe you do want to keep it local. Almost any other type of product or service you will want to start investigating national or international advertising almost immediately.

b. **Failure to maintain a website** – This goes with advertising for two simple reasons. First off, most folks, of a certain generation, can't even find their phone book, instead they will flip on the PC and try and find out something about you or your products through the web. Therefore it truly is a valid component of your advertising model. But that's not where your ideas will stop. Because next, and possibly most important your website is going to be your 24 hour a day store. You will have contact and product details, you will have and post press releases, you will be listing special deals and sales as well as perhaps creating a repository of additional and ancillary information that your customers can return to over and over. Now they will be coming back to your website regardless of exactly what they need.

One thing that I would like you to promise me, or better yet yourself, is that you will not fall for the line by **anyone** selling you advertising from any phone book, which then follows up with, "Of course we also will develop a free website for you!" Free websites are worth exactly what you pay for them. Worse, since their primary business is telephone advertising, they will offer you one of "6" templates to use for your website so if there are 30 companies like yours in the areas, then 1 website in six will look just the same!

Now there are entire books on Advertising, and even more books on advertising on the web, add to that the number of books that are available on how to write a website, then add on the books that teach you how to use your website for business. You know what you get? A lot of reading. Seriously, using just those 4 categories, Amazon shows over 62,000 different books. I think even a Nook with 64GB of storage may have a hard time carrying that many books. So lets just talk about a few basic ideas.

First, one of the most popular uses for a website is to advertise your company, your product and information about both. The next most popular use is as an order method for buying your products and services. But in order for that to happen people need to know something about you! Which in turn leads to advertising (see why were addressing both here).

There are as many different thoughts and ideas about how and what to advertise on the web as there are people in NYC. So, what do you do? How can you make sure that your new business with its new products, becomes the most talked about thing anywhere? Ten years ago you could have spent a *million* dollars a week on buying ads during "Friends" or whatever the current TV Show is, but is that really your best use of resources? Probably not.

The bottom line is, unless you are already an internet based advertising guru, you're going to need some help, which means probably spending a little money. So how can you make sure that you are investing as little as you can in the right places? Well the easiest method would be to ask someone who is either in the same or at least a complimentary business. Next I would say, check out your local Community Colleges, there are hundreds of folks on campus who want to use their talents and could use a few extra dollars at the same time. Using a resource like that you get the latest ideas without having to mortgage the farm!

Next of course comes what **type** of website do you need? Again, my opinion remains the same, most "free" websites don't do their jobs well for business (if at all) therefore you will want to learn how to find your own hosted site and work from there.

Finally will come the question of What *kind* of website do you want? I have found that currently Wordpress has such an active support base right now, with so many different themes, widgets and designers that if your willing to look, you will find the one you need. However as with other websites, the free Wordpress sites are much too limited to be of really good use to you the business owner, so again look for your own hosted site.

With a little research you can find an excellent hosting company that will cost you as little as $25 a year, and then the balance of your investment is between you and your webmaster.

7) Not protecting your Assets, Personal and Business.

Unfortunately we have all seen the story, about the mid-western High School teacher who gets fired after a photograph of her performing an act "unbecoming an educator" is found on her Facebook page. Or the one where the Football coach is fired from his dream job as head coach for his Alma Mater because a video of a similar nature is found on YouTube with him wearing the team's jacket. Technology is great, especially if you're an administrator and need to "rein in" some folks. But that's not really what we are looking for here, or is it?

One thing that I advise all my clients is to understand that you are on public scrutiny alert 24 hours a day. Every now and then, at least once a year, go to one of the better search engines and type your name in and hit search. The first time I did that I found a series of technical articles that I had written more than a decade before the internet even existed! Try it, let's see what you find. Because the folks that you want to do business with? Yeah they can do the same thing, more importantly, more and more of them are doing exactly THAT. So don't get caught with your pants or anything else down.

The point that I want to make is that no matter what you call it, your reputation, your dignity, your standing, your profile or just plain old integrity, protecting that is worth almost more than anything else I can think of in today's business world. You are going to be working with many folks who may never get the chance to meet you, much less 'get to know you'; therefore your first impression is not just vital it is crucial. Protecting what your customers, clients and co workers are going to see is something that you need to be on the watch for every single minute of the day. I recently heard a very successful businessman say "The Most important dollar in your business is the one that you use to protect your integrity." I believe that whole heartedly.

So when folks are talking about 'watching your assets' they do often mean, to make sure you have enough insurance, but they are also talking about those intangibles. The things that can not be replaced or re purposed. Once it's gone it will take years if ever to build that back up in someone else's eyes.

Protecting your company's physical assets is fairly simple; however the best way that you will ever find to protect your companies' non physical assets are to have a very good and very liberal return policy. Now if you are selling a physical object like a TV or computer, you have the manufacturers warranty to rely on, then you can actually create a larger perceived value of your device if you ad on a 1 year unconditional money back guarantee! I understand that in the face of it this sounds very expensive, but the $1 you give back may be the best investment you have ever made. There is a whole prison full of "business men" who were going to "be right" and went to jail for fraud rather than give up a few Thousand dollars in refunds.

Now if you are a service or some other type of business, the real "loss" is in your time. You may be able to create a great deal of wealth that makes your per hour figures look very good but the $100 you 'save' by not giving a refund because they are on day 32 of a 30 day warranty is going to be very expensive. Please, protect the integrity of your business, it doesn't take much, and in the end, it doesn't cost much either!

8) Personal Expectations are too High

I have a training session that I give in many of my classes called Gen –x and the attitude of **Entitlement**. Somewhere along the line my generation has given the children who are now business aged the idea that everything is theirs, and that yes they can be president when they grow up one day. As matter of fact the country owes it to them. That type of attitude is going to make it very hard to be broke and still go out and wash Fido behind the, well Fido's behind. But that is the attitude and the expectation that you must maintain a firm grasp on, or you will find yourself sinking your own ship.

The reason I repeat this section is because it leads into something that none of us like to talk about, and that is "Lack of Success." Yes I know most folks call that failure, but that is such an icky word isn't it? I mean really, look at it. Look at it long and hard because there are going to be several nights where you feel as though that's the only direction you are moving.

I recently read a short Biography on Winston Churchill, and what most folks probably don't know is that like many others, he suffered from extreme bouts of depression. The difference was, he recognized it, and searched for a way to deal with it. What he found was that ,"The best way to defeat the black dog is not to feed it!" In his day there was no psychological diagnosis of depression with its resulting pills to make you feel better, so he called his, "the black dog." In his opinion the best ay to defeat the black dog was to starve it, the way you did that was to stop feeding it wrong questions, and start feeding it right questions. Questions that will get you out of your problem.

Instead of saying "How am I ever going to meet payroll this month." Ask yourself "What is the best method for me to exceed my expenses and make my payroll with abundant profits?" They are both questions that are trying for the same answer, but one is said in despair and is demonstrating the lack of confidence needed to actually reach that goal. The second question is already assuming that you will meet the goal and instead just wants to make sure you use the best methods to pay your employees from your profits as they should be, instead of trying to find the money from some other source!

9) Not Solving a REAL problem

You have got the idea of the century, your brothers, wife's sister – in – law knows this butcher who made a gnosh for a guy one time who...and now you have a product, or service that you are sure will sell a million units this week! Oh yeah? Says who? You and your ego or the hundreds of people you've heard complaining about this problem that you think you can solve.

You need to evaluate whether or not your business ideas solve a real problem or addresses a real customer need. Then ask yourself if there are people out there actually looking for what you plan to offer, and how much they would be willing to spend to get it. Now the one nice thing about buying a business or a franchise is that you have the confidence that the master company has done the research needed to make sure that this is the right business for the right location.

But don't bet on it. Take a little while, talk to your neighbors. If you bought a Hungry Louie's Pizza franchise and there are 17 other Pizza restaurants in the same neighborhood, what makes yours stand out? Alternatively if you decided that nothing goes better with everything than bacon, yet immediately across the street is a Kosher deli and on the opposite corner sits a Mosque and your property is actually owned by the SDA Church, maybe you have the right idea, but the wrong place!

Did you hear about how NASA spent millions back in the '70s trying to make a pen that worked in space? The Russians gave their astronauts a pencil.

10) Lack of FOCUS

This could, and perhaps should (see volume 2.0) be an entire chapter, but for the moment lets work with the space allotted. I recently drover by a Taco restaurant, they had replaced their sign. What had been "Jocko's Taco's" was now "Jacques Famous French Cuisine and Taco bar, featuring the Fresh Catch of the day!" HUH? It's like that kids show from when we were all little, which one of these things doesn't belong together? For grins I stopped in and asked the young lady at the Hostess stand (now that was new too), when the sign had changed and how business was.

Her reply pretty much said it all, "Well when it was Jocko's Taco's everyone knew what they were getting when they came in. Ever since Jack came back from his honeymoon in Cannes, no one knows what they will see on the menu. Can you believe he actually tested out an escargot pizza?" Yes pretty young lady I can, I have seen this happen far too often. The small Irish immigrant mistakenly receives tickets to a Snoop Dogg concert and now he wants to know where he can put his 'grill polish.'

It's typically men, of a certain age, but honestly it can strike anywhere, anytime and involve almost anything! Unfortunately its usually the moderately successful businesses that suffer the most, If you are like me you're already pursuing several projects because it appears that one will not suffice or if you have several then surely one will succeed right? Umm, no. Choose one of them and focus on it. You will be amazed at the clarity of purpose you discover along the way, and if you determine that this is **not** the path you should be on,. At least you will have examined it very closely and carefully.

When have you ever focused on several things and done truly well with all of them? Make sure to test them individually before you make a decision to add one to what you currently have, but choose one as soon as possible and stick with it. There will come a time and place when you will want to expand what you do, year one, may not be the best time to try it.

Your best bet however is to find folks that may have a vested interest in you or your success, and who have been involved in owning a business. Personally I'm not going to ask my friends, family or anyone who has never been in business. Those kinds of folks are going to look at you in one of two ways, both "biased." First they will answer as though your still "little Stevie" from down the street, that sold cub scout cookies as a kid. Next they will look at you as though they were your protective warrior. They are going to look at your business as though they are going to protect you from something, and no matter what you show them they will look at it as though you will be throwing money in the street. Your best bet, ask your potential customers. Then once you know if they want to buy your product, ask the folks who are mentoring you. Your mentor has a vested interest in seeing you succeed, but not a relationship that is so close they cant see the reality.

5. Why are you doing this again?

At This point its NOT for the MONEY.

Remember earlier when we talked about the types of folks who decided that they wanted to be entrepreneurs? Well one of the things that we didn't really talk about in depth is this; Why do you want to be or think you can be an entrepreneur? So lets take a break for a minute and toss some ideas around and see which one fits you the best.

Why do you want to be "on your own?" Your answer to this question actually reveals a great deal about where you are in your business development portion of your life, but lets see where you think you are and compare that to where you should be if you want to keep up your sanity.

Believe it or not, there are a lot of folks, usually the younger ,and more energetic among us who immediately respond with – money! At which point the older, more seasoned and experienced business owners try to stifle a smirk. See you can decide that you want to run your own business for a lot of good reasons, but money is not going to be one of them. Maybe its because you know that you are the only person in the world who will truly pay you what you are worth! That's not a bad reason. Maybe its because you have an idea that you just know you can translate into and extremely successful enterprise in a short order, but the idea is so selective that it only takes one person to execute the idea! That could even be considered a good idea. I would even be willing to accept the idea that you have developed such a unique skill set as to be able to help folks one on one and truly bring about a positive change in their lives. That one I will accept.

Now let's talk about some really bad ideas for wanting to start your own business:

1)   **Money** – You knew that was coming first right? Think about it though. If you have read the other books in the *"Remote Control Career"* series you know that there is a "motivation" tool used by management that I believe is a poor substitute for real desire. That tool is to throw money at your employee and hope that they will stay on with you. This is almost the same idea but in reverse. You are in a Thirty Thousand a year job and because you don't believe you have any other marketable skills you see that as the only way to increase you income. First off, that's a really bad idea, and has very little foundation in reality. Now if Great Uncle Louie died and left you 4 million dollars and wants you to buy a sandwich shop franchise, that's one thing, but if you are going to use whatever savings you have to start a hot dog stand on the weekends, that's not such a good idea, for several ideas. First, according to the SBA almost 95% of all small business in America fail due to lack of planning. Money is part of the planning. Second many companies who have a great deal of capitol may take several years to turn a profit. Even the Mega site Amazon.com took over 5 years to turn a profit. So the real question is, how long can you tread water? I mentioned earlier that you should have at least 6 months worth of your expenses (that's you bills) in the bank before you

start. That is with the understanding that the goal is that within 6 months you would plan to be able to pay yourself enough to meet your bills. But what happens if you don't? I know a young lady who mortgaged not only everything *she* had, but her parent's retirement fund in order to start her own business. Twelve months later she decided that it wasn't worth it anymore, the stress the struggle, the plan just wasn't working. So she liquidated everything she could and went back to work in probably the toughest industry available. Now I'm not saying that her **only** mistake was not having planned out a profit plan, there were dozens of holes in her plan, my question to you is this: When the going gets tough, the leads dry up and you have to decide whether you are paying the light bill or the phone bill, will you carry on?

2)   **You HATE your job** – I won't hire someone under the same circumstances, so I can not with all good conscience recommend that you start your own business. First things first, determine what it is about your job that you dislike so much, then see if you can fix it. If you still want to be your own boss, maybe it is time. But whatever it is that has soured you on your job, find it and fix it. When I have someone who is looking for a job and they make any indication that they are dissatisfied with their current work environment, they automatically go to the bottom of my list. It's not that I won't ever hire them, just that the pickings would have to be awfully slim. Much like the money motivator, the 'newness' of a new situation,

whether it's a new job or your own business, will wear off rather quickly, so once the 'newness' has worn off, then what? Your "anger" at your old boss is **not** going to perpetuate you through the hard times. The idea of you powering through the famine just so that you can prove that your former employer was wrong is not something that happens often in America, not outside the movie theater anyway. So if you don't like your job, decide what it is, is it the career, the corporation, your individual manager, or, do you honestly just have that desire to go out and do your own thing. You may not be able to fix the things that are bothering you, but at least you wont be dragging them around like an anchor.

3)   You KNOW you can make a MINT – This almost sounds like number 1 but its slightly different. In this case you are leaving your current situation because you have an idea that "can't fail to make a million dollars the first month." In other words you are going into business not because you want a business of your own (but you do, so you don't have to share the profits), your not trying to better anyone's situation, you may not even have a better product/service you are just looking for the bottom line! I was coming back from a conference when one of my companions started talking about how "little effort it took to do that." When I asked him what he was talking about, I mistakenly thought he meant come up with the concept we had been trained on. No, he meant put on the training seminar we had just come from. What he saw was 1000 folks taking a day off, each paying $49 a head to listen to some training to help them do a better job in what **they** did, and then subtracted out what it cost to rent the hotel room etc. A few weeks later the grand opening of "Big Boys Seminar Promotions INC." was well under way! He saw, that on the surface, something 'looked' easy (after all isn't that how all of our customers should see what we do?) so he determined that he could make his $10,000 piece of the pie! Instead, six months later, the website was gone, the business cards were boxed up and the phone was disconnected. The good news is that he really hadn't invested much money, but he had lost the one thing he will never be able to get back, his time. He had started a business on an incorrect premise, using insufficient data, and learned a great deal in the process. Actually he should have learned a great deal in the process, unfortunately 6 months after that...

4)   It's a GREAT time for me to get started, and after all it is all about me - It is a sad but true fact of life that in some cases Entrepreneurs can be some of the most self centered egotistical folks on planet earth. (I know I was one of them at one time) To be honest though that in and of itself is not a negative for your business. It may not be especially good for your customer service but as long as your customers will support your attitude more power to you. However if you have just gambled your families entire financial future (at least the next several years of it) on an idea that is "too good to fail" then you may as well start sending out resumes today. No idea is too good to fail. I have seen business models that have had everything that you can imagine going for them, but the owner didn't do any product/project research and the business fell right through the floor. Just because now is a good time for you does not mean that now is the time that the rest of the world is waiting with baited breath to buy what your selling. Have you done your research? Have you tested your products viability? Have you even done a search to see if there is something out there like what you want to do?

Most folks are so scared of someone "stealing their idea" that they keep it wrapped up in a deep dark closet and dare not whisper anything to a soul until launch day then they are amazed that no one is beating a path to their door with wallets open and currency a flyin' . I'd love to tell you that, this is the one sure fire way to become a success, but unfortunately its only a sure fire way to the poor house. First of all competition is not a bad thing. How great would it be if there was only one other source of what your making/selling around and it took them 4 – 6 weeks to deliver where as you can do the same thing at the same price point in 4 to 7 days. Now you have folks running in your direction. Afraid to show anyone your idea for fear that they will "steal it?" Most people are not that ambitious. More importantly they will, in all probability, look at what you have done and go "well I could do a better job than that." Then roll back over and watch the end of the Simpsons. Research is your best friend when your idea strikes. Get on the web, gather up the trade journals, head for the library, find out if there's anything like your product and if there is, how your product is that much better! Besides if you ever get the idea that your business is all about you, it's time to find a new business.

5)   Because you want independence, complete and total independence - Everyone wants a piece of your success and no one wants to help with the work, but this is in no way a solitary business. Even the "ancient texts" will tell you that you need to develop a "Mastermind Group." When Napoleon Hill suggested, almost 100 years ago, that you develop your own 'Mastermind Group' he used his own example of a fictional group of famous figures upon whom he had done sufficient research that he felt he could almost "tap into" their knowledge base in order to come up with all new alternatives to his own issues. Today you don't have to be nearly so creative, in most cities and towns of any size you should be able to find a group of like minded folks that you can meet with on a regular basis and confer with, both on your issues and some of there's. If on the other hand you should happened to be located in some remote area that has no networking groups or where there are absolutely no products or businesses like yours, remember, there are national organizations that generate and have Global Mastermind Groups. These types of groups however are typically very specialized very picky about who can and can not join, and typically there will be a fee to do so. One such group that I am familiar with has a very exclusive mastermind group with some very interesting registration requirements. Their fee to join the group is a 3 year commitment to $10,000 per month. Each member must be generating no less than $1 million dollars net each year in business and they will only accept one type of business into the Mastermind Group at a time. So if you're the Dry Cleaning King of Sandusky OH, and you are accepted into this group you will be the only Dry cleaner owner in that group. Many folks don't understand the advantage of this, but once you have experienced the major differences that someone who is not familiar with your business can and will make about your business, you will quickly determine that this is the only kind of group you want to join.

Now if you reflect on history you will note that Napoleon Hill did indeed conduct a Mastermind Group while being completely alone. But if you do your research you will find that this was not by his choice, but he was the originator of the term and therefore had no way to explain or demonstrate that it not only worked, but worked in his favor. So if you think that being in business **for** yourself is an excuse to be in business **by** yourself you are very much mistaken. At the very least find yourself one person that you can learn from and be accountable to. It doesn't matter what your business is there will be someone somewhere near you who has the experience to help make your idea a smashing success.

The challenge is are you strong enough and committed to your own success enough to truly open yourself and your business up to this other person? Leave yourself open so that they can give you the guidance you need? Again you can have the greatest product paired with the most amazing marketing plan that the world has ever seen, but if you are the only source of your own ideas, things will grow stale rather quickly. Not to mention the well known fact that it is much easier not to do than to do. Therefore let your mentor be your accountability partner as well. Develop the kind of relationship that you respect them so much that it hurts you to disappoint them on the off chance that you don't succeed. Also make sure that the relationship is "pure enough" so that you won't fall into the trap of "fudging" the facts when telling of your successes. If you can't be honest with your mentor, then you're going to lie to yourself just as easily.

So please, while your doing all your planning, or in some cases "re planning" make sure that you're not trying to be a "lone wolf", wolves hunt in packs for a reason. There is strength in numbers, even if you are just using your numbers as a resource to bounce ideas off. You will find that not having to carry all that stress around by yourself if worth more than you can even count.

Now that you're depressed, and almost completely talked out of going into business for yourself, what are some of the right reasons to go into business for yourself?

After all there are billionaires all over this and other countries who started a business for themselves and have had great success with it. So with these things as being really good reasons not to go into business for yourself, what would be a good reason to go into business for yourself?

A) You will be able to get many things done faster: But not everything. Have you ever had an idea that will save your company a million dollars, or so it seems, and so you work on it over the next few weeks at night, draw it out, address as many of the objections as you have ever seen come up and then finally take it to your manager and proudly say. "This is a million dollar idea." He looks everything over and agrees, this is great and it will save thousands if not millions on the bottom line, so he takes it to his manager.

You hear nothing about it for almost a year, then suddenly an email comes out from on high thanking good ol "John Horowitz" for creating and implementing an XTZ system, that looks very much like your idea, but has so many operational holes in it, that no one bothers to use it! Thus it dies a slow and unkind death while good 'ol John H. gets moved right into the 3rd floor along with the intending bonuses and promotions. If that doesn't ring a bell, either your not old enough or your not trying hard enough. I remember making a suggestion at a Sr. level meeting once, being greeted with lots of agreement and then watching the whole thing be executed so poorly that it ended up costing the company Ten's of Thousands of dollars. In that case I was very glad to see that someone else took the credit.

But, in your own business, as the CEO,CIO,CSO and BOSS you will have the opportunity to implement your ideas with immediate swiftness. Assuming you didn't do something stupid, like issue common stock, you are still the end all, be all, voice of your company. So you will be able to take those ideas and insert them into an operation mid stream, if that's where you feel it belongs. However make sure you do your due diligence. You can implement changes in your marketing strategy post haste and probably not kill your entire business (Free Whoopee Cushion with every order).

But you also don't want to over promise and then find out that its so expensive, that just turning the idea **off** will cost you all of your profit. Always give yourself an exit strategy in anything you do, and if you are trying something completely new, work on a 'split test' where you have a "control group" of 100 customers who remain "as always", then you have another 100 customers and you implement your new plan. Now statistically speaking in order to get your percentages as close to perfect as you can you really need at least 1200 customers in each group, but you'll work it out, just don't try your whole customer base at once. Or you may find that you have difficulty finding the first 100 customers for your next idea.

B) Control your own Life and Business: I almost erased this and placed it in the previous section. Many entrepreneurs that I am know seem to be more controlled by their business, than the other way around. The nice part is that it does not have to be like that. With a little proper planning and some foresight you can run your business on your schedule and still have your lifestyle, while creating a profit.

Now the first way to make sure that you own the business and it doesn't own you, is through establishing right up front, the proper customer expectation management systems. For those of you with your own business you know that this can be done in many ways. It can be as simple as setting a realistic return/refund policy or developing a pre set method of how and when your services are available. Obviously if your business is supplying motors to heart and lung machines, you will probably need some sort of 24 hour response line, but my thinking is, if no one is going to die and no one is going to go bankrupt then how much of an urgency is there?

This does bring up a very crucial point that must be addressed up front and that is establishing, in the beginning, a working relationship with your clients that sets up good customer expectations. This should include an understanding that their forgetfulness does not necessitate an emergency on your part. Unless they are willing to pay.

I have a very good friend who owns a very successful business selling something that could almost be considered a luxury item, although there is some security tied in with it, and when they are assembling the system it is explained to the new owner that there is a regular maintenance schedule that must be maintained for proper functioning. Unlike changing your oil every 15 – 30k miles, if you do not change your batteries in your remote control, you will not be able to enter or leave your home. Yet, approximately once a month he will receive a screaming telephone call from a client whose system "just stopped working."

When asked about maintenance they always seem to have just performed it. He very carefully explains that if the problem is with the product its his cost, if the problem is maintenance related they will be charged an emergency service call fee. Amazingly enough after they are made aware that the fee for the call would be in excess of $500 many of his clients suggest that perhaps something else might be the issue, and no longer require him to come out. Those remainders typically only have to pay that fee once, before they start checking their batteries before they call. His goal with setting the fee at that point is to encourage folks to think for themselves, discourage needless interruptions to his home life as well as make sure the customer is aware that this is another person with a family that they are talking to, and certain considerations should be taken by both parties.

This system was not always in place, he placed it there after his seventh year in business when his wife explained that his business was getting in the way of his family life, not making it easier. Although many of his 'competitors' were sure that this would mark the end of his business, what he soon found out was that most people have enough common sense to not want to disturb you, the rest just need to be reminded. A little planning on the front end will relieve a great deal of stress on the back end.

C) **You are in control of who you will and won't work with:** In many cases this is true, unfortunately it does depend on the type of business you own. For example, in almost any non corporate store, you will find a sign to the effect of:" *We reserve the right to refuse service to anyone.*" Now as far as I'm concerned I agree, if you own a pizza shop and you don't want the local food critic coming down to eat at your restaurant, you should be able to ask him to leave. Unfortunately in today's litigious society that is absolutely 100% un true. If you own a pizza restaurant and you post a sign like that, let me list some folks you should never apply it to: anyone of a different race, religion, creed or color than you, anyone younger or older than you, anyone taller, shorter, fatter or skinnier than you, and finally please do not be fooled into thinking that all handicaps can be seen. They can't. My own father for example, would look hurt if you offered him a seniors discount, yet demanded it, if you didn't.

I worked with a company once and a gentleman was hired for my team who was very severely handicapped, but unless he chose to reveal it to you, you could only 'see' one of 3 handicaps that he endured. We were lauded as the most wonderfully open minded and progressive team in the corporation. Unfortunately he didn't work out, it had nothing to do with his physical issues and everything to do with his being a bully to other employees when I wasn't around. Two weeks after he was terminated the company was served with a lawsuit for handicap discrimination. Now , how he found a lawyer to even accept his case is a matter I dare not enter. I will say that after 2 years, he was told, after his final appeal, that he had no case, and should have accepted 2 weeks severance pay. But the idea is this, some folks will attempt to use to their advantage anything and everything that is within reach, in order to collect a *big payout*. However, as with #2, with a little planning and forethought you can almost 'hand pick' 100% of the folks that you choose to work with, as long as you have established the rules up front.

    a.   The easiest method is through your business design itself. If you don't care to work with a certain group of people, lets say you only want to deal with the wealthy, then design your business so that your products and services are not only affordable to the wealthy, but by the exclusive nature, they are really only attractive to the wealthy.

b. Alternatively you may also find that the very nature of your business lends itself to only one particular type of person and not another. For example, if you enjoy 'open minded' folks sometimes portions of the Real Estate community or an entertainment industry could be where you should aim. However in some areas, neither of those groups are really known for having deep pockets, so if you have several smaller ticket items you have a better bet of generating a return.

c. In almost any type of 'target marketed' business in which you are not having your initial contact face to face, you are much more open to picking and choosing your clientele. I know a millionaire several times over who will tell you without even flinching that if he could manage his business without ever having to see, speak with or hear from, one of his customers he would be much happier. This is an absolutely brilliant individual who just has no tolerance for people. Some types of medical professions lend themselves to the same type of situation.

D) You take the risks, you keep the rewards: This is almost 100% accurate. You will absolutely be the one person assuming all the risks associated with your business. However, the part about you keeping the rewards, lets talk about that for a minute.

Your business is selling custom left handed widgets to folks who have had to endure adapting right handed widgets for over 20 years. Sounds like a pretty tight knit group that would be easy to sell to, right? Possibly, but folks, especially southpaws, who have had to endure aggravation for an extended period can become rather inventive.

I once knew an auto mechanic who specialized in one particular brand of auto. He would work on anything but if you own a Zubelwagon you went to Tim. The one thing you knew about Tim though was that all his knowledge was obtained the old fashioned way, experience. He had taken apart and re assembled more Z-wagons than any 10 techs in America, but he didn't have the time or the money needed to attend their certification school. The nice part about this school, apparently, was that upon graduation you received an official set of ZW tools. Tim didn't have these, so instead he had an entire toolbox full of 'regular' tools that had been bent, twisted and somehow misshapen so that they would fit inside the z-wagons engine. Many left handed folks are the same way.

But you have developed not only the widget, but an entire line of support implements to go along with it. Now you just have to get all the current owners of widgets who are 'mis-using' their widgets, to hear about yours. While your at it, getting information about your widget in front of the folks currently looking for a left handed widget would be ideal. Does this sound like advertising? Because it should. So now you must create an advertising budget, but before you do that you probably should perform some research to find out what's available for who, and where they all live. This could be an entire series of investigative and research costs in and among themselves.

So you beg borrow and buy every manual available on marketing to specific subgroups, and you are confronted by the fact that the average cost of acquiring your customers is going to run approximately $12 per customer. If your widget only costs $14 you need to do one of two things. Either have some type of "back end" product that can be upgraded for the customer after they own your widget. Or you could raise the price of your widget. All of this, the research, the target marketing, the potential redesign of your product, and or your back end, add up to increased costs of customer acquisition which must come from somewhere.

I recently spoke to a very smart, very rich man, who's initial product to his customers was $197 item. He then explained that in many cases the cost to acquire that customer could be as high as $250. I'm not sure about you, but where I live it appears as though he is 'losing' almost $53 per sale. He agrees that in certain situations that is exactly what he is doing. However, the lifetime value of that particular customer, who starts with his $197 item averages out to approximately $4,200. So in his particular case his up front costs are very high, however his 'lifetime' income from that same customer is almost 22 times that cost. Now the $4,200 figure does not apply to 100% of his customers, but it applies, in his case, to customers to make more than 1 purchase every 6 months. Statistically this would apply to 20% of the folks he contacts. So in the end it all works out.

But what if he had not planned to lose that $53, most small companies couldn't afford to lose $1 per customer if it were not expected. Now this particular gentleman was not just starting his business, he had been in business for quite some time. He actually started his business by selling a $49 product whose production cost was $6 and his acquisition cost was less than $20 per customer. But he also admits there were days when he had to either sell more than one product or not have the gas money to go home. Yes you do get to keep your profits, your net profits. We haven't even (nor will we) begun to touch on taxes. I will suggest this, do not attempt to avoid paying taxes. The cost of you owning a business in America is that you will pay some taxes. How much you pay should be left to a competent CPA.

E) You can follow your dream/passion: Absolutely true. However you also must be sure that your dream doesn't become your nightmare. Once again this is completely in your control and can be worked out ahead of time, with but a simple bit of planning. One thing you should always plan however, are vacations, but more on that later.

What is your passion? What is your hobby? What is your dream? These often can be tied together, and often can be turned, quite profitably, into a very successful business. In *"Remote Control Professional"* we give the example of someone who likes to play the guitar, and the many options available and how they can be spread out, but lets try a different tact this time, Today lets say that you have a burning desire to feed the homeless. Well I think that right off the bat we could probably all say that there is not much profit in giving away food. There may be grants and loans and other assistance items, but not any profit that immediately comes to mind. However lets see if we can find some:

Primary Passion: Feeding the Homeless:

1) Is this something you want to do completely on your own or would you be willing to team up with another organization?

2) Do you have some area of specialized knowledge currently in demand: Whether its fixing PC's or speaking in public or teaching a foreign language.

3) **EX**: *Speaking in public*: Offer free classes on overcoming fear while giving presentations at your library/service club.

4) Record these presentation both on audio and video, for later re-packaging.

5) Create a small mailer with your BIO and why you can teach business men how to give better presentations every time.

6) Mail this along with a CD/DVD out to every service club president in your area, and offer to give that presentation. Church's are also good venues.

7) Create a very low entry point/fee for teaching this to small groups or individuals

8) Mention that a large percentage of your fee will be going towards the "Speakers for Meals" program that feeds the homeless.

9) As you start to present to more service organizations, many of who's members are business owners and VP's will invite you in to larger venues.

10) Once you obtain enough money from your percentages you can now buy the food needed for the next meal or next holiday meal for your local homeless shelter.

You have now achieved your passion. Albeit in a roundabout way, but you have succeeded, both in creating a business and in investing back into your community.

As a side note, almost every personal investment manual worth the paper it is printed on will tell you, from all the funds you take in there is a certain percentage which should be "given away" often referred to as "sowing seeds" back into your community. Most of these manuals will also refer to no less than 10%, but obviously if this is your passion you will feel compelled to sow even more!

There you have it 5 good reasons **not** to start your own business and 5 good reasons you should start your own business. Truth be told the reasons for starting your own business so far outweigh the reasons against, there is absolutely no comparison. Our goal here is just to try and give you as many opportunities as we can to see things as absurd as they can get, so that you can approach them with as clear thinking as possible.

But in the end it really is up to you, what are your reasons for wanting to be in your own business? As long as you approach them with the same clarity and dedication as you have in almost everything else you do, you will be a great success. Not everyone is born an entrepreneur, but so far I haven't met anyone who can not learn how to become one.

5. Education

Finding out what you don't know

We now know **what** we want to do, we even have a pretty clear idea of **why** we're going to do it, now lets take a minute and talk about learning **how** to do it. Most folks will start a business based on one of two concepts: Either they already know how to do what it is that they want to do because they have done it, **or**, they have just gone to school, (college or franchise school) and learned how to do it.

Both of these are great ways to get started, and in both situations you are performing a task based on knowledge that you, yourself have acquired. Now there is a third option, and that's called doing something based on what someone **else** knows, you'll find out more about that technique in the book ***How to create a $50,000 a year job from a $1,000,000 investment***.

The one question that you want to start thinking about, even before you open your doors, be they real or virtual, is where will your continuing education come from? I know a lot of folks just heard a brain cell go 'pop' between their ears. Yes, you invested all this time and money and effort obtaining the education that you have to start a business, why in the world are you worried about continuing education before you even open your business? Well let me ask you this, would you rather have a brain surgeon who goes to the Brain Surgeon Institute of America , graduates and yet is willing to learn new techniques every year, or have

71

one who graduated twenty years ago and has been working 'just fine' without all those extra classes? For my money, more education is better, and no mom that's not just because I spent 10 years in school (sheesh some people never forget).

So now you understand that continuing education may be something that you want to invest in, what do you study and where do you go to learn it? Unfortunately that truly depends upon what kind of business it is that your developing. No, that's not a cop out, really, here's why; some businesses include continuing education as part of their package, and most require that you decide to go out and find your own.

For example, there is a gentleman here in the US who offers continuing education classes that range anywhere between Five and Ten thousand dollars per course, usually a 3 – 5 day course, for folks who have decided that their passion in life is carpet cleaning. I kid you not, go Google "carpet cleaning seminars" and I guarantee his will be on page one. Amazingly however, his will not be the **only** one, who knew?

On the other hand, I met a guy at the fair a few years ago who painted "Outer Space-scapes" (his term not mine) using krylon and trash can lids, and claimed he made about $100,000 a year doing it. You and I both know that there are art schools on almost every street corner, certainly on the back of every comic book. But I think this guy is probably so busy making money that he wouldn't have time to go to a 'traditional' art school.

So if you were Mr. $100k artist, what kinds of continuing education would you look for, and where would you be able to find it? First you have to understand that the very nature of his business makes enrolling in a university or regular college class tricky, after all his business is in Boise one day and could be in Milton the next, so unless you want to lose that coveted parking space, this is going to take some planning.

That's exactly what it will take, if his earnings statement is accurate, then one would imagine that he probably could afford to take at least one week off a year, not counting vacation time. I'm not really sure how the "fair circuit" works, but I would believe that it, like most businesses is rather seasonal. At that income level and his age, which I neglected to mention was under 30, my recommendation would be that he learn how to diversify his income so that when he decides that he's too old for the road, he has some choices. Now he needs to find some seminars, in the fall and winter that will teach either something very diverse, real estate investing, or something that could be compatible with what he does, forex trading perhaps?

Here is what I know about both of those businesses, they can both be done anywhere in the US, and in the case of forex trading, really the only requirement, other than cash and knowledge, is a consistently reliable computer and internet connection. When it comes to real estate investing some of America's biggest millionaires became that way by investing in areas outside their home neighborhood. If his fair is traveling the country one would imagine he is passing hundreds if not thousands of opportunities daily.

Now he has determined that he needs a fall or winter class, better one in each season, in either forex or real estate, how does he find what he needs? That, of course is the million dollar question. How can you tell the **good** information providers from the **rip-off** artists? Not to say that there are a lot of folks looking to steal your money, but lets say that because of time considerations he really doesn't have the time to do a lot of trial and error.

I would say that it is similar to looking for almost anything that your going to invest in, the criteria will be the same. You're going to invest your money into something, whether its an education or an antique airplane, and you hope that at the other end of the process you will find a way to make it profitable. So what would be the first thing you might do, if you were going to invest in something, but you weren't an expert on that something yet? No not ask dad. In most cases that is the last thing that you would do, however, along those same lines, find someone whom you do respect and get their opinion.

In this case our spray can artist wants to find someone that he knows or has respect for, who does have knowledge in trading on the foreign exchange market. Now, if you are a spray can artist I mean no offense, but lets say for examples sake, that he doesn't really hang around in circles where this type of specialized knowledge is handed out freely, where would he go to look? There are some traditional sources he could try and some sources that are becoming traditional, lets look at those.

1) **Local Newspaper** – Most major Metropolitan newspapers will have a finance columnist who could be a good source of information. I say 'could be' because one has to really examine where one gets the information he will use to invest for retirement. But if your local paper has a finance column, look through a few weeks of it and see if he even mentions what it is that you want to invest in, if he doesn't directly he may mention someone he would recommend, or he may list his email address. If his email is part of his column, drop him a line and ask where he gets his information.

2) **Syndicated Radio/TV –** There are as many radio and TV talk shows about money as there are about Asian Bass flying around Lake Michigan (that's a lot). Pick one you understand and can relate to and follow him or her for several weeks. Again they will undoubtedly, **not** be handing out advice over the air. Legalities , lawsuits and all will normally prohibit this kind of thing. However, they will undoubtedly drop the names of some of their information services. Also in the case of most nationally syndicated hosts you will find that they have large web sites that will have information for sale and often times they will have forums where their fans get together and talk about and trade ideas on what? Yup, financial advice, and those folks will be begging to hand out free advice. You of course are smart

enough to turn your BS filter on high, knowing that sometimes free advice is worth far less than you pay for it. Best of all however this leads us to our third option which is...

3) **The Internet** – This is the free trade of information for the entire world. If you are a fan of free speech, this will be your heaven. Unfortunately if you are brand new at what you're looking for, this can also very rapidly place you in information overload. The way I used the net for my searches will not be something that everyone will do, but it's a pretty good idea that many folks could benefit from.

    a.   Register for a 'free' email account from Gmail, Yahoo etc. Most of the sites and people you will be researching will want an email address. Trust me, save yourself a lot of aggravation and cleaning, and do not give your main personal address.

    b.   Install a new Internet Browser on your PC. Like your email, you don't want to 'clutter up' your main browser with all your "new" information. I prefer Firefox and Chrome, but there are dozens.

    c.   Search Google for your Niche, whatever that is, and use the "advanced" search tools to get as absolutely specific as you can. If you have determined that you want to learn Foreign Exchange Trading. Use not only those words but terms like, beginner, education, mentors.

    d.   Run through your search results *very* superficially, every site that even looks remotely like it could apply to you, save it as a bookmark, but place some in a bookmark subfolder called **initial search** or something. Devote about 2 hours to your 1st search.

e. Now, dedicate another 2 hours to **begin** sorting through what you found. Look for 2 things. First look for sites that have *very* active user forums, that way you can ask questions and get answers from many users. Next look for one that speaks your language. If you don't know anything about the exchange you do not want a site written by a Harvard MBA.

f. Save the ones that meet that criteria to another folder marked **forexsites** or something you will recognize.

g. This is the one step that everyone neglects, but devote at least another 2 hours to looking at each of the sites you saved last, and find out "who" is behind it. There are typically one or two folks generating most of the information. Keep written 'log' of these guys' names. (WordPad or notebook will suffice)

h. Now you're going to start some 'negative searches' take the names list you created and feed them into your search engine, and if the advanced search will allow it, take out their own website references, and perform a search. What your looking for is dissenting comments. Claims of 'rip-offs' 'fraud' and 'no help' are things to look

for, but take them all with a grain of salt. You
really are looking for any legal claims.

i. You should now have a list of 4 – 6 good names
of folks who, per your research, not only should
know what their doing, but that you can
understand.

Register with those websites, dip into their forums, and
spend a few days, an hour a day at least, reading everything you
can. Some of it will be junk, some of it will be sales material, but
you will start to see through exactly who is making money and
who isn't. This is definitely one of those cases where you want to
'follow the money.' Typically on almost any subject I will find 3 –
4 web sites on my own and then be referred to 1 or 2 more as
you start to add to more value to the discussions that you are
following. Don't be afraid to comment or ask questions, just don't
try and be an expert because you read "Forex for Dummies."

I'll be honest, I don't know much about forex trading, other
than as I said, most folks I know who got started, did so slowly
and used money that they could afford to lose. No one I have
ever met has ever suggested "Go sell your car we need the
money for this deal." My Dad always said "if it's a good deal
today its going to be as good or better deal tomorrow." So far he
hasn't ever been proven wrong on that idea. Plus very often
anytime I have tried "too hard" to make a deal happen it has
turned out to be far less than expected.

4) **Traditional School** – One would imagine for an artist on the move, that this, would be an impossibility. Or is it? If your only view school is of checking into a college campus for 4 to 5 classes a day 3 to 5 days a week, semester after semester than you probably right, it's not a good idea.

But what if your not 'on the move' yet, maybe you're still living at home, or with some friends? Well now you're going to want to visit as many educational institutions as you can find, and interview their art departments. Most folks in the art world that I know are pretty savvy with what they do and do not know, they understand where their weaknesses lay, because everyone is willing to tell them. So when you start looking, look for programs that cater to those weaknesses, even if you have to interview the individual instructors themselves.

Now I can already hear it starting, "But I live in XYZville we don't have anything like that here. You think not? You would be amazed. I live in a city of less than 2 million and we have (within 20 minutes driving)no less than 6 branches of state colleges, 2 state universities, and countless private colleges. Not to mention 3 major private art museums all of which have 'art school' attached to them. That's just from a scan of the yellow pages. Again, whether they cater to what you're looking for or not, only you can tell. In the early 70's I knew a guy who went almost 1000 miles to attend a specialized art school. Now the Junior College in the city he was living in then had a similar program for far less money.

But, OK, for a minute, lets say that the' on campus' life is not one that you can sustain, or that can sustain you. Can you attend a remote learning course of instruction? Don't laugh, people have been attending the "Art Institute of America" by drawing a squirrel they found on a matchbook in a bar for longer than I have been alive. I'm not lending any credence to that institution, but I do know if you can spell it, someone offers a course in distance learning that will teach it to you. This does not even include the opportunities that videos and DVD's have brought to distance learning. Bob Ross taught on PBS for decades and his classes will be running for decades more, now that he's no longer with us, and I have seen for a fact the idea that some people can and do learn very well that way.

5) **Mentors –** One of the most vital pieces of the puzzle would be finding someone else who is doing what he wants to do, and learn from that person. 100 years ago you would be called an apprentice and at some point in your early teens your family would make arrangements for you to go live with a "Master Craftsman" for X number of years. He got free labor (your room and board were negotiated ahead of time) and you learned a craft. There are still some very select groups of craftsman who work this way, and some unions have a similar program, although I don't believe that even I have ever heard of an apprentice program for "Spray Can Artists." But one thing I have learned over the years, if you can imagine it, someone else out there is willing to teach it

to you from his 'years' of experience. The other half of that statement is that you will end up paying for those years and years if experience.

In my own life, I was riding back from a conference one Saturday, suddenly the guy sitting next to me turned to me and said "heck *we* could do that, if only we knew how to X." Well it took almost 10 years but suddenly, during a presentation one day, a gentleman that I had known for many years, yet lost contact with, approached me and offered to teach *me* 'X'. Needless to say I snapped up the opportunity and have been thankful ever since. It's amazing what some humble attitude and proper guidance can do for you.

6) **Study at Home** – Finally we reach one of my favorite methods, as from my experience there is nothing that can't be learned this way, its easy enough to sum it up by saying ; books, tapes, cd's, dvd's and seminars. I have utilized these methods for over 30 years and have not found a subject yet, from guitar playing to Linear Algebra, that can't be learned this way. I used to be under the impression that not everything was able to be communicated through this method, but that's back when I was only choosing one. I would read a book and not feel like I got "it." Or I would listen to an entire series of tapes and still feel that 'something was missing.'

It was only after I started being smart and combining these methods that I could see how it all came together. Believe it or not, for me DVD was not the best way to learn music. Only after I combined the videos with some good illustrated manuals, did it all start to come together.

Most folks dismiss this type of learning as too funneled or not 'broad enough' or worse yet, 'painted with too broad a stroke.' When I query most of these commenter's on how they connected with their education, they would typically comment that it was through one single process, as opposed to combining them. Now when you're combining your methods you may find that combining your teacher's works best for you, and in some instances seeking separate instructors for each technique may work best. Taking our spray can artist as an example, he may find the greatest videos in the world that teach "How to use Krylon." Yet still be unsure as to how to combine that knowledge into something that resembles a spacescape. So now, he may be looking for books or magazines or, something else entirely.

7. Required "Ancillary Skills"

So far most of what we have talked about are ideas and skills that you needed to turn your ideas into a business. However, you will find that as your business gets going, there are certain skills that you will want some familiarity with, so you have an idea of what's going on. Yes there are zillionaires who claim they outsource everything and don't know anything about anything other than their specialty. I believe that these folks are leaving a lot of money on the table, and earned the majority of their money before 1999. Why 1999? Because the majority of these skills are technology based. I'm not suggesting that you need an IT degree, just some familiarity with what's going on around you.

1) Blogging

Believe it or not this has become a huge part of business today, as well as a key component of making sure that a business gets it's name "out there." Most search engines are being programmed today to look for repeated references on key terms made by the same websites, and that's how they formulate their rankings (this is a very basic explanation). Therefore if you own "Bob's Left Handed Shoe Supply", the one sure way to guarantee that your companies name keeps coming up in the right searches is to update your website with information as often as possible. Unfortunately that can be a time consuming job, and definitely takes some skill. If however Bob publishes a blog and 2 – 3 times a week writes a post that is of interest to folks who are looking for a supply of left handed shoes, his companies name and information will come up more and more often. The best part is that almost any tablet pc and many smart phones now allow you to post to your blogs.

Two things I would be wary of in running a blog, the first is outsourcing, again there are lots of people who say that they 'elance' everything. My opinion of these blogs is that if you know anything at all about the subject, you can spot the ones being outsourced, not to mention the language issues that could be involved. Secondly there is an entire series of software available for sale and rental, that will take, for example, an article that you wrote on waxing left handed shoes, and "re – word" it into 3 – 4 different articles. All of which can be re posted all over the internet to keep your name on the search engines. Once again, the results vary, but unfortunately everything I have seen as a result of these applications, is awful and obvious.

2)   Open Source

Now I admit I'm an open source advocate, and I am not suggesting that you toss everything from a retail store or large corporation and start over, I am suggesting that you not become 100% dependent upon your vendors support. It can be very expensive plus they are very rarely available when you need them most.

I have had several clients whose businesses have almost ground to a complete halt while they waited on technicians to come to the rescue. In many cases there are cd's available with alternate operating systems with complete office suites, that would allow a business to continue to be productive while waiting on their technicians. Check out the "resources" at the end for a few recommendations.

3) **Web Manipulation**

I used to put programming in this slot, but whenever I did one of two things happened, first folks got scared and shut the book, or people went off the deep end learning the ins and outs of C++. Since the majority of a businesses 'presence' is in some way web involved now a days, you, as Chief Cook and Bottle Washer, should have some familiarity with how your website works. Even if you were smart enough to pay a local high school kid $10 a day to setup and maintain your website, prom week you wont be able to reach him.

So when someone calls your company, like I did just this morning, and asks for a piece of information, that is clearly available on your website, and I say "Yes but that part of your site is not available right now." You will have some idea of what to do. No running in circles setting fire to effigies of Bill Gates is not the proper response. Although there is a time and place for that type of thing. If your 'web resource' is the only one who has your login ID's and passwords, you have placed yourself in a very precarious position. Even if that resource is a relative, things happen, intentional things and things that are called mistakes, the worst of those of course are classified as 'natural disasters.' The sad fact is, they happen, just not to you, right? Most of these issues can be resolved with a book like "Web Sites for Dummies" or even a free library class on building your own site.

4) Hardware Familiarity

I once knew a major mortgage broker, this man had been in business for decades and he always wanted to be on the cutting edge of technology. Unfortunately all his education was in banking and finance. So although he tried to understand everything, there were things that he did in setting up his office in which he should never have been involved. It took time away from what he did to generate income. If computers are not generating income, than you should not have to have yourself in them elbows deep. This broker was so enamored with his own knowledge he was often seen 'saving pennies' on purchasing his computers while spending thousands of dollars in support. Probably not the best use of his time, or money.

On the other hand, there was a small business that used a "Pak and Ship" concept, you know bring your 'stuff' to them and they did everything including file insurance claims if something got lost. She was as scared of computers as a mouse is of a lion. As such she refused to go into a computer store for anything, instead she continually purchased anything and everything from friends relatives and garage sales. Not the best IT strategy either. Find a happy median, where you know what you have, you know what you need and there is a balance there. As I tell my 5 year old, the difference between what you want and what you need is a lot of money.

5)   Social media

Depending on who you talk to Twitter, Facebook and YouTube are the saviors of the Internet, and the only way business will be done in 5 years. Of course I think that 5 years ago it was Web 2.0, MySpace and Flickr, but I could be wrong. The idea is that Social sights have proven their worth, but very few people have proven how to generate an income using them as anything other than another billboard. This does not exempt you from being aware of these services and how to use them to your best advantage.

In each case there are bright yellow books that will walk you through step by step getting the basics down, and if a book is just too darned much information to digest at one sitting, there are some wonderful UK magazines publishing "special editions" each of which is devoted to getting you up to speed in the briefest format available to you. If this is the route you take I must warn you, you can't think of these as buying another copy of INC. magazine, when you find out they cost anywhere from $15 - $25USD you will appreciate the information as well as understand that they are being shipped across the ocean. I could devote entire chapters on the different aspects of social media and how to use them for your specific business, just understand that if you do not have a presence in these areas there is an entire generation that will not lend you any credibility at all.

The cancer institute in my town has a Facebook page. When I saw that announcement I thought it was the biggest waste of 10 minutes I had ever seen. Then I thought about it from a business perspective and I understood. They are not looking for advertising for their hospital or their doctors, instead they are looking for "image advertising." That's the kind of advertising that many companies never even consider until some product or employee causes some huge natural disaster. This is called a "preemptive" strike.

6)   Web Design

In most cases this gets lumped in with the 'social media presence' or 'web manipulation', but it really needs to be a category in and of itself. Again you don't need to understand the ins and outs of CSS, HTML5 or JAVA2, you do however want to make sure that you, as the business owner, are consulted on what goes into and makes up, your web presence. As we talked about earlier more and more people are using Google than are using the white/red/yellow pages every single day, and if your web site is slow, unreliable or boring, you may as well stay in bed every day.

Unlike the manipulation mentioned in item #3, we are far less concerned with the 'keys to the kingdom' per se, and here we are looking at what the web site looks like, what it says and the information it puts out. If you have a blazing hot news item about your Christmas party with photos, for Christmas 2007, you are going to get talked about, just not the way you want.

Let someone else do the hard stuff, if you can imagine it, someone can figure out how to do it. I would warn you however that flashy bright moving stuff with loud noises or videos with soundtracks that start automatically, are a one way ticket to a closed browser in my office. Nobody wants to advertise everything that they are searching the web for. Your customers are no different. Give them some exciting options, give them some cutting edge, but let the option be theirs, not yours, as to when it starts and at what volume! Most of all, make sure that your layout makes sense, I was setting up a new 'gizmo' that required me to use the manufacturers site. When I got there, there was nothing that said 'start', 'enter' or anything else, just a big swirl and the companies name. After 30 minutes on hold I was told that I was the 20th person that day, who "didn't know you just had to click on the swirl…" If I'm number 20, that day, I have to wonder how many tens of thousands that month, never bothered to call, except to return the gizmo?

7)   Accounting / Bookkeeping

Please understand I am **not** suggesting that you necessarily want to be your own Accountant, you do however need to be able to read a P/L statement as well as keep close tabs on your invoices and outlays. My recommendation is that the moment you cross that threshold where it will affect your income (traditionally $3k a year or more) you go find yourself a good bookkeeper or accountant. There is a big difference between filing your taxes as a W-2 employee and filing them as a self employed business owner. Additionally if you have actual sales of goods, that will typically involve the filing of State Sales tax (sometimes city and county as well), all of which you should be able to find in one book keeper.

How do you find your book keeper? Well if your son, cousin or Uncle Mortimer took night classes in accounting, let them find their own business you're not there to be charitable. If they press, just explain that as complicated as things are 'about to get' you certainly don't want them to risk their business just by accounting yours. Therefore take it outside. As in many other cases your best bet is to talk to other folks who do what you are doing and ask who they use. Many times you will find that the best small business accountants are taken, especially if you wait until March or April to start looking, so look early or look late, don't wait for it all to hit.

Additionally, find someone who understands what it is that you do. For example if you will be retailing and wholesaling pig manure as 'organic' mulch, you are going to find that there is a much bigger difference in paperwork alone between filing information on the two businesses, than most folks imagine. Also your tax structure and collection schedules are much different for your retail and wholesale customers as well.

8)   It's all about your people

If you keep your ears open, and do everything you can to learn as much as you can, you will undoubtedly hear a certain group of businessman tell you that your job as a business owner is to earn every dollar that you can, in every way that you can. I know some of these folks personally, and I am confident in saying that they do not run their businesses as callously as this may sound. However I think we need to emphasize this by taking it one step farther. The value in your business, in any business for that matter, lies 100% squarely in your customers. It's not your list, its not your marketing, its not in developing your next whiz bang product. Without your customers none of the rest matters. Now the question you have to nail down is exactly **who** your customer is. We will get into descriptions later, but first lets say we know who the customer is, what do we need to do to make sure they are our customer for life?

Surprisingly one of the most 'callous sounding' businessmen I know says flat out that in his business, "If someone asks for their money back, we give it to them, no questions asked." Far be it from me to try and shoehorn you into a business model where "the customer is always right." In all honestly there are some cases where he isn't. If you happen to manufacture small arms, and one of your suppliers comes to you and says he wants a Strawberry Cupcake Revolver in Bright Pink, don't even *ask* who he is going to sell that to, and just ask that he go somewhere else.

We cant regulate people, but we can monitor our interactions with them. So when you look at your customers, and your products, if you just think through the people aspect, and I mean all your people not just your customers, then I believe you will find that there is a much better business to be involved in, than the one your first saw. Remember, even if the core of your business revolves around owning a "u-store it", you're not a warehouse owner. No, you help people preserve memories for their future generations.

9)   Never bombard people with your business

Young, old, new or experienced, you can tell when someone has just started a new business, as my aunt used to say "Your not changing my mind, and I'm not changing the subject." That is one sure fire way to drive away potential prospects faster than anything else in this world.

When I was involved in Network Marketing, the old joke was 3 things are faster than the speed of light, Telephone, Tele friend and tell anyone your in an MLM. Regardless of what your opinion of that particular business model, the fact of the matter is, it earned that reputation, the hard way, one overzealous distributor at a time.

The reality is that not **everyone** is a perfect fit for your business, nor, contrary to popular belief, does everyone *know someone* who is a perfect fit for your business. There are very easy ways to work your business into almost any conversation and **not** make you sound like a rabid dog. We will cover this more in some detail in a later area, but find yourself a good set of questions and keep them at the ready. Questions that make you seem interested and not creepy.

For example, whenever I find myself in the proximity of a woman that I'm not friends with yet, it seems as though small talk is expected. I will often start with, "besides maintaining a home, what kind of work do you do during the day?" That lets her know that I give credence to home makers, yet I understand that in today's economy most folks perform more than one task.

If in the company of a man the question is similar, but with a quick follow up: "So John, what do you do during the day?" Let them answer, then reply with; "Really, how did you get started doing that?" You are now the number one conversationalist in the room, and everyone, at the end of the night will remember how great it was talking with you. Why? Because you were interested in them.

Now on the off chance that you know what they do, you may begin with ,"John my new company moves me in a lot of circles that are different than I used to be associated with, on the off chance I happen to find someone looking for what you do, describe your perfect customer." Again your asking about how you can help **them**. In the majority of cases they will turn the conversation around on you and ask you the exact same question, and that is your opportunity.

10) Learn how to speak more effectively

An amazing statistic was recently unveiled during an international survey: over 95% of every Business Degree offered requires some type of public speaking course, if not more than one. One of my favorite realizations in college was that Tech Writing which is what many folks used to get out of speech class meant writing a technical presentation every week, and then presenting it before the class. Seems like speech class would be easier? Unfortunately most of the instructors in most of the speech courses that I took, fell into one of two categories. Either they were frustrated English teachers who didn't have enough classes to fill, or they were the lowest man in the Theater Department, and therefore had to teach speech.

I will be the first to admit, I honestly believe that in 9 or 10 speeches you can significantly improve your methods and manners of speech. However, that's assuming that there is someone 'different' evaluating your speech each time. In a speech class, typically the only one evaluating your speech is the instructor. The problem with that is that you're getting one persons opinion, one viewpoint on how things should be done. You may come out with an excellent command of the English language and still stand as stiff as a board, at least when your not gripping the lectern in abject fear and panic. Just because they are a great English teacher does not qualify them as a presenter, and just because they can recite sonnets in their sleep does not mean that they have a great grasp of the English language. Look for a balance. If need be seek out someone else in the class whom you feel is a good presenter and ask them to evaluate your presentation. Toastmasters anyone?

11) Success is neither immediate nor imminent

One of the hardest things I have to do as a success coach is prepare folks for the fact that their success is not guaranteed. Some folks, when they do come to that realization, need to understand that even when success seems within reach it may not be happening today. Now I'm the first person to tell you that if you put your nose to the grindstone and work like mad your success has a much better chance of happening than not, but sometimes all you end up with is a ground down nose. This is why researching your business before you ever start is not just a good idea now a days, it's a requirement. If you should ever get to the point where you are approaching a traditional bank for funding, the first thing that they are going to want to see is a demand for whatever it is that your 'selling.'

But, since we're smart Entrepreneurs and we understand that the 'new tradition' of starting your business with someone else's money isn't working so well (ask the folks at pets.com), we won't even be considering that angle for years. But what is it that we need to focus on as far as our success is concerned? That's the easy part, as that should be planned and laid out in your business plan, you know the 6 – 12 month plan, the 2 – 5 year plan and the 10+ year plan.

In those plans lay the seeds for your success, as well as the outline of the one thing that absolutely every single person ever to develop a successful business in America in the last several hundred years has known, and that is to have patience. We would all love to wake up tomorrow and have 'Good Morning America' clamoring for an interview and the Wall Street Journal telling the world about how we went from failure to success in a little less than 15 minutes. The challenge with that daydream, is that it has absolutely no basis in reality.

When I was in the Mortgage industry I considered myself fairly successful at what I did, as did most of my peers. But the two things that most folks didn't know about my career in the mortgage business is #1 I started as the computer guy, and got the chance to be a broker because they were shorthanded. Next, I knew that *what* we were doing, *how* we were doing it, and the *environment* that we were doing it in, was very unusual and was not built for long term profitability. I was in my first mortgage company, as a broker, for only 19 months. I generated a great deal of income for the company, and then sold it to my partner. Unfortunately 6 months later he was broke, the economic climate that he operated under had changed, and it was determined that his business was now being developed around **one** very important factor. The challenge with that was that when that factor changed the very foundation of his business was no longer valid.

Similarly, in the early 2000's all you had to do was add .COM to the end of any string of letters or words and people would almost throw bags of money at you. No I wasn't in that business then. (I kick myself quite often for missing that train) Again, the businesses were not established for long term profitability or stability. When you are Apple, and you have 20 years of business behind you, go ahead put a basket ball court in the conference room. When you're bubba.com and you don't even have a product, you probably should be putting some of those funds to better use, like maybe finding, buying or developing a product?

12)   Sales without income are called ideas

Actually they are considered liabilities, but most Entrepreneurs won't get to that level of accounting for several years. But in reference to all the .com busts of the 2000's Entrepreneurs now found that they had to contend with many "new" issues. These new issues seemed to be in addition to their "out of control spending." These other issues revolved around selling products without collecting funds, and using those sales as a basis for 'growth.' I worked with a very large IT firm once and although it was hard earned, and hard for them to learn, they did determine that regardless of how many 'letters of intent' were signed, until

97

silver crossed palm, there was no sense in increasing the workforce.

I distinctly recall one instance where a project was announced, the press was called, parties were planned and champagne uncorked. Somehow, in the following six months all reference to that project slowly faded from view. Finally in a departmental meeting someone new asked the question 'What about the XYZ project?" That person received a very stern look from her manager, and although no one knows for sure what went on during their closed door meeting later that day, this employee never uttered a word about that project ever again. Sometime after I parted ways, I ran into one of their Sr. Managers and found that their customer had made many promises, not only of what they would pay, but that they could pay, and yet nothing ever materialized

13) Shortcuts are for short timers

If the business you're planning on going into will be something that you hope to sustain for 90 days or six months? If so, shortcuts probably won't hurt you too badly. However if you plan on this being a long term business, as you should, than you need to understand that fast this and over night that are thoughts, ideas and phrases to be avoided. If you have a mentor, as you should (see our section on education), that person should be the first person in your line up that will tell you that there are no shortcuts.

If that person is encouraging you to take shortcuts they need to be replaced pronto. Short cuts are fine when your 6 and your looking for a faster way home from school. So you cut through the woods and snag your pants and step in a stream. By the time your opening up your own business those same kinds of shortcuts can turn into long term nightmares. I wont single any specific company out, but I think that if you search out "man made disaster" in your favorite search engine you will almost always find out that someone somewhere in the chain of errors tried to 'save time or money' by doing something that they shouldn't, and ended up causing a cascade of events that created the issues that turned into the disaster itself.

There is a reason that the 'old timers' from the 30's and 40's talked about 'the struggle' and 'the fight', in those era's you occasionally were required to roll up your sleeves and get physical. Not that you were involved in a bar room brawl with your suppliers, but when someone didn't show up for work, guess who got to unload 170 cases of roofing nails. Right, whoever it is that's standing around waiting for their next assignment, and when those folks were all used up it came to the boss man himself. Either pitch in and do it, or lose the job to the next younger, faster guy who could get it done.

14) Money is easy to spend and hard to earn

Treat it with respect. Earlier we talked about some of the wasteful spending that many of the .com companies did in the 2000's. Just as harsh was the Mortgage broker who was his own IT guy, and instead of fixing a problem, bought new hardware or software to fix it for him. But it doesn't even have to be anything as dramatic as that. I worked as a manager of a Finance Office in the late 80's, the boss hired his 'main squeeze' to help open all the new offices for him. Typically these were not brand new, from the ground up type of new offices, these were offices that were taken back from franchisees that couldn't make a go of it on their own.

Therefore the 'office' itself was functioning, but was not turning a profit. So when he told his girl to 'clean house' that's exactly what she did, literally. She would take his corporate charge card and spend the morning throwing away every piece of office equipment and stationary item in the office that was not nailed to the floor. As she did this she made a list of what she threw away, so that the afternoon was then spent at the office supply store buying replacements for everything that she had just thrown away.

Now I understand that if the name of a business changes, you really shouldn't keep the letterhead with the old name. But the first time I saw her throw away a trash can, only to buy a brand new one, identical in everyway, I had to say something. What it came down to was, every time this gentleman was assigned a new office, aside from any and all acquisition fees and retraining rehiring he had to do, he needed to factor in almost $7,500 in extra charges. In his view, he left 'that part of the business' up to her, and she said it was needed, so he went along with it.

Unsurprisingly enough, several years later when this same young lady, who was now single, wanted to start a business of her own, she developed a great business plan, she went all the way out 5 years, I was so proud. When she showed up the first day with 2 brand new mini vans (she had no employees and no clients at this point) along with new custom interiors and custom paint and signs, 5000 pieces of custom stationary, all in beautiful 4 color I might add, I was speechless. If we were in a classroom I would ask for volunteers on how long her business lasted, instead I will tell you that she personally filed bankruptcy in less than 16 months, a filing in excess of over $280,000.

15)   Treat your competition with respect not contempt

I have heard many very intelligent business folks make the statement, "If your product/system/etc, is good enough, than you have *no* competition." Now I do believe that you may have something that is so unique that folks may not have to choose between your left handed all feather covered widget and someone else's. But if your widget is just another way to open a bottle, guess what, they are already out there.

But lets not even get that specific, go up one more level in the development chain, what does your widget do? Let's say for examples sake, that it solves the number one complaint that most house wives have about cleaning their ovens. So you are selling a 'fancy' oven cleaner, in the larger perspective. Well there are other folks out there who also sell ways to clean an oven. They may not be as slick and clean and pine scented as yours, but they are out there. So yes you have a unique product, you even have a unique delivery system, real feathers, but the bottom line is, your customer has **x** number of dollars set aside for their cleaning budget.

You and everyone else out there in the market, which has some product or service that could fall under those same parameters are in business for the same dollars. They are your competition. Treat them with respect. For several reasons, I'll give you the top three here:

    a. You do not want to start a 'turf' war. If you happen to be going up against a multinational conglomerate with very deep advertising pockets you do not want to go head to head, you will lose.

    b. Until you have established your brand and your product as a genuine solution to this problem, you do not want to attract the attention of certain folks. The government, late night talk show comedians and regulators of any kind.

    c. Finally, if your product is going to be marketed to "the greatest generation" or anyone near it, anytime you choose to "knock" the other guy, you choose to make yourself look bad. Plain and simple, that's how they were raised, it needs to be how you do business.

16) Your home life comes before your business life

There was a period during the 80's when the push was for financial success at any cost, hopefully we have seen enough of our colleagues suffer from heart conditions and other ailments to understand that a more balanced set of priorities is a requirement. The most common method of stating this is that you can make all the money in the world, but if you have no one to share it with, what does it matter?

Unfortunately entrepreneurs are the folks who are most likely to make sacrifices on the home front in order to succeed in business. Worse yet, business is not the only way that entrepreneurs get out of balance. I had a meeting recently with someone who is very big in my specialty and in relating a story about a mutual business owner that we had both helped on different projects his observation was, "You know I told John that competition is good, but he needs to focus his priorities."

It seems as though John had joined a service organization that had contests that he felt would help him get his name out, so instead of spending his weekends working on his family and on his primary business, he was suffering the repercussions at home and at the office of too much competition. So sometimes its not just your business that gets in the way of your life, or more directly its not 'exactly' your business, but as far as your family may be concerned it may be related to business.

17) You are not the only one with your idea.

I did a presentation in college once which traced every modern invention, this was before the advent of PC's, back to a toothpick invented by a guy named Ug. As fanciful as that may be, there are very few product or service ideas that you may try and put into production today that truly are original. Really, that's OK, as a matter of fact if you haven't, and you should have, done enough due diligence to find that other product, I suggest you give it a try. When I suggest this to some folks they get very defensive and immediately try and explain why theirs is so much better than anything that may have come before. But that's not why I want you to do the research, I'm suggesting that you look to see what may have come before so that you can study what they did and did not, do right. There is a great deal in business to be learned from history. Not ancient history of foreign civilizations, but the history of business and commerce in your country, and more importantly in your business.

This is just one of the reasons that I suggest to everyone that they study as many business biographies as they can. Even if you garner only one business idea that you can use in the future, that one idea can be worth millions. Just as a clue, when I was in the real estate business I had just finished reading Donald Trump's first book, the same chapter that made me realize that he was a financial genius also gave me an idea that secured almost 3 million dollars more on a deal that I had been working on for over a year.

18) Secrecy rarely helps

At some point your going to advertise your product, business, system or idea, at that point the cat is out of the bag, so telling your father in law a few months before launch date will undoubtedly not cause the end of the product. If it does, than maybe there was some other research that should have been done? The internet has allowed a great many things to happen all over the world, but as far as I can see one of its greatest benefits in the business world is the ability to test an idea and research the results of others at little or no cost.

Now I will be the first to say that putting a wild and wacky video on YouTube once you have launched your product is a great way to get free publicity from the late night comedians, unfortunately getting that kind of attention before your launch could be a negative type of attention that you don't want. However sharing your idea, at least within your own circle is a great idea, if for no other reason than accountability. Whether you are writing a book, or developing a car that runs on lima beans, you will have a set back. By sharing your ideas with those around you, you can find the support you need to help get you through such obstacles. Accountability, it should be a chapter on its own, but even if it's not, you will find it more important than almost anything else in your business.

19) Media coverage is really fun, but also a huge distraction.

Some folks tell me that for someone who promotes interaction with PR as a part of your business plan it's a little strange to say that the media can also be a big distraction. But I think that we can all agree that we have seen many folks, both we may know personally, or just see/read in the media. They 'get famous' and then their 'product' suffers.

Just as an example. There is a gentleman who customizes Motorcycles, he got a TV show, married a starlet, got divorced, lost his first TV show, started a second one, and now, no longer owns his Motorcycle shop. Now there could be a number of reasons why that is, but I would imagine that when dozens of pro sports figures are paying you a quarter million dollars a piece for custom motorcycles, you probably can't say it wasn't a "profitable" business anymore.

Alternatively there are some folks who have very successfully harnessed the power of national media attention to their benefit. There is the head of a particular advertising agency on wall street who was asked to judge a project on a "reality" show and now his company handles dozens of accounts for some of the biggest ad buyers in the world. What many folks may not know about this particular man is that in the 90's he ran a 'direct mail' company. That's where he got all his great copy writing practice. Writing ads to sell you his own merchandise. He sold his marketing company, opened another company, and then through his association with one of the largest financiers on the planet, became known as one of the greatest "ad guys" ever.

He wrote books, went on speaking tours and did consulting for thousands if not hundreds of thousands of dollars. But again, this wasn't his first experience with the media, he had dealt with them as a direct mail owner and as an "ad agency", so he was very familiar with their tools and tactics.

20) Your business plan will change.

One would almost think that this is a redundant statement, but it astounds me at how many entrepreneurs become 'married' to their first business plan, and do everything that they can, to resist changing it. Now I don't want you to drop your vision the minute a challenge sets in, because you will have challenges. Again, this is a given, but chances are also great that if don't allow yourself some flexibility in the beginning of your plan, then you may not have anything in place ready when you need it. I suggested at one point that when you lay out your plan you need to make sure you have an exit strategy, even if that strategy is to just drop your current production plan and start from some entirely new direction.

I know a young lady who decided that in her town, which was heavily populated by tourists in the spring and summer, that she would maintain her business year round, unlike some of her neighbors who closed up during the cooler months. Now this may not seem revolutionary, until you look at what and where her business is located. You see she has a specialty restaurant in a 'coastal' town. In the winter there is some snow skiing and ice fishing for the residents, but once summer hits, it becomes a beach town. Every *other* season she did great, in the summer it was hot dogs and beer and in the winter it was hot chocolate and mulled cider.

Unfortunately in the Fall and Spring the tourists went home and she was dealing with the locals. Most of whom were not attracted to her 'boardwalk based' café. However, once she changed her menus and offered 'free delivery' she found that it really was just a natural extension of what she did 'in season', and that employees from all over the county would call her. Additionally it did draw some of the locals back to the boardwalk. Being an astute business woman, she made arrangements with different businesses to sponsor local bands and from about 3pm until 10pm, allowing everyone on the boardwalk the opportunity to make money year round.

All because one business person decided to change her business model instead of just giving in and taking "half the year off" , she was able to increase her bottom line by over 30%. Additionally, as some of her business neighbors watched her success they too decided that maybe they didn't need all three months of vacation. Now the boardwalk is for locals all year round.

21) Change is inevitable (and necessary)

Now understand change being necessary does not make it any less painful, it just means it will happen with or without your input. However I have found that one way to make it tolerable is to include my input. Thus attempting at least in some small way to ease my way through the entire process. The best part about this idea is that knowing change will happen means that most of the things that you do to prepare for it, only make it easier.

Note I said most of the things you do, not all of them. However I can assure you that the one sure fire way to guarantee that change is painful and excruciatingly slow, is to try and hide from it. When we are small and we see something that we don't like, often times we will 'freeze up' and let Mom and Dad deal with it. Unfortunately this same attitude becomes part of some folks 'make up' and even well into adult hood they try the same tactic. This time they find themselves on the wrong side of a situation with little if any time to do something about it.

The good news is that when handled properly some change can be seen in much the same way that the rains meet some parts of the Savannah. To an outsider the sudden downpour of buckets of water that strike with such force that the ground can no longer soak it up. The same torrent that results in a flash flood, that sweeps the plains clean, also give everything a brand new beginning. Now I'm not suggesting that you need to fire everyone and start over every time a change occurs, instead when a major change appears on the horizon, and you find that you, and your business, are not prepared for it, look at your processes and procedures. Look very closely. No one expects you to be a fortune teller, but is there anything that you could have changed or a process that could have been altered that would have either allowed you to avoid the change or at least come through it unscathed?

Now is the time to look at your business, your plans, and yes, even your staff, and determine what you need. Then compare that with what you want. Any spot that the two don't meet you have some decisions to make. Either the plan changes, the process change, or the people change

22) Your customer database is your #1 asset

If you ever reach a point in your business where selling the company is an option, as a whole or major portion, one thing that every financier and investor will be looking at is your customer catalog. Specifically they are looking for things like 'cost of acquisition' and 'return on investment.' Yes, the same thing that Wall Street looks at in "Bob Mart" the smart investors are looking at when examining your business. Where did your customer come from, how much did it cost you to get them and what kind of job have you done in keeping them happy? The easiest way to measure that particular statistic is, how often do they come back and what is their re-order rate? Are they spending more, less, or the same every time they order.

If their average ticket isn't increasing with every sale than one of three things has occurred.

a. You didn't treat them very well

b. There isn't a great deal of value in your products, from their perspective

c. Your prices are too low.

What do you think is the easiest one of those three that you can change without affecting your profit margin? Well in many cases value can be tied to quality, or perspective. Unfortunately it often takes an application of funds to change either of those. Your prices may be too low, in which case the only way to find out is to test a different price strategy. But the absolute easiest way to increase your companies' value in the eyes of the customer, is by treating them better.

This will begin every single time the customer walks through the front door or calls you on the phone. Who is their first contact? Are they knowledgeable, clean, and neat in appearance (or do they sound that way?). In one of my previous companies we had to deal with a vendor on a regular basis through their "Customer Service" phone number. Every single time one of my folks would hang up they would compare notes to see "who they got." Even the most courteous of my team would comment that "if she had to deal with Zelda again, she would just hang up." My team had dealt with these same folks so often and received the same reactions time and time again that they had taken to nick naming everyone they spoke with. Unfortunately, for the vendor, none of these names were complimentary in nature. When asked to describe Zelda, one team member said, "Oh you know, she's morbidly obese, sitting in front of her TV, smoking and eating, and apparently we are interrupting her soap opera's." These folks had developed this from a repeated series of 2 minute contacts with this particular vendor over and over again.

What nicknames has your staff been given by your customers, more importantly, why?

23) Know your ideal customers (inside and out)

There is a concept in business today that is directly tied into this idea, but may be taking it a little farther than most folks are prepared for in the beginning. I'll take a few steps back and then touch on the advanced before were done. The bottom line is, before you start your business, or as soon as you possibly can, take the time to determine "who is your ideal customer?" Now I know we all want to say "Everyone is, everyone in the world needs what I have to sell!" As true as you may want that to be, chances are I can find one or two folks who will just not fit your description of a good customer. Or, and this is something that most entrepreneurs are not prepared for, you may have a particular customer or type of customer that you do not want to deal with.

So its up to you to really step back, look at your product, or whatever it is that you're going to market, and determine what is a valid and concrete description of my customer? More importantly, how well can you refine that description? By that I mean, the finer you can focus your customer list, the better overall experience you're going to be able to deliver. Let's use the example that we have now:

In our previous chapter we talked about becoming a "Spacecape artist that uses spray paint medium" Now I think that for a business, that is a great step at narrowing down exactly what your business is. You are not an artist, your not a portraiture artist, you're not a landscape artist. You are specifically painting Outer space oriented landscape paintings using common spray cans of paint. So who is the ideal candidate to buy your product?

1)   Folks with cash to spend. Unless you want to get into 'financing art' and there are so many things wrong with that I won't even begin describing them.

2) People who collect art. Although you may sell to someone who doesn't own any art at all yet, the chances of you making a high dollar sale as your first sale to someone's collection are rather slim.

3) People interested in Science Fiction. Sci – Fi fans like to buy things, and most of them are interested in artistic things. This Is from personal experience.

4) People interested in the Space Program. Again folks who like NASA generally appreciate art with a space theme.

5) People who have purchased space themed art in the past. If they will buy once they will buy again.

Now you have a pretty specific idea of who your customers are, and who to market to, now you need to figure out a way to find them specifically. Imagine, if your selling $2000 worth of art every month by working County Fairs and local Art shows, how much more art could you sell through a direct marketing campaign aimed at people who have bought that style art before and, because of your "Gallery" on your web site, now don't even have to leave their home in order to buy more. We will cover how to find these folks and reach them in our chapter on marketing, but your getting very close.

24) Every business needs an exit strategy

I am not talking about how to move to Antigua with all your profits when the FDA tries to shut you down. But again, looking at our example, there may come a time when the fumes from the paint cans have gotten so bad that you no longer even recognize the dog, how can you leave this huge Artistic Empire that you are teaching folks to create?

That's what we mean by having an exit strategy. However the other may be something that you want to keep in mind, just in case. Imagine, its now been twenty years, we have generated a business that is comfortably bringing in $250,000 a year, between our 'how to videos' , lithographs and endorsements, your married and your kids are just about ready to move out, its now time for you to give your sweetheart that long delayed honeymoon trip around the world. How do you STOP working? Aside from the health risks that many entrepreneurs run by retiring, what do you have that's going to give you that last one big investment so that someone else would want to come in and buy your business?

As we discussed previously, your biggest asset is your customer information, and no I'm not suggesting you start renting your customer list so they are inundated with "draw Sparky" brochures. But what do you have that you can place a value on that would actually generate an offer? If you have kept good records you should have a great database full of customer contact information that lists what they bought when and maybe even some why. You also have 20 years worth of artwork that you've stocked for lithograph or ancillary sales programs.

What are ancillary sales programs? Well you know how the Beatles songs were used to sell some sneakers? This is a similar idea, but instead, your going to license your artwork to be used in films and book covers and advertising work. Also you do have that "how to business", maybe it's a few videos and a book, although after 20 years one would truly hope that you have an entire "training system" developed that you can now market. You can tour art schools and college campuses talking about the various ways you've generated business and ideas.

Are you seeing how you can retire and not lose your income? That's called having an exit strategy. Now if you want to sell the business and act as a consultant or public "face", that's up to you. But at least now you're not inhaling paint fumes for the next 20 years. You now have in place one kind of a residual payment system setup to keep things running smoothly for yourself and your family. The biggest shock to most entrepreneurs comes after they stop working, a total cessation of activity. Unfortunately most entrepreneurs don't prepare for that well enough, and that lack of activity, that lack of stress, is what leads them to and early grave.

8. Focus

Whether you like him or not, it would be very difficult to argue with the fact that Donald Trump is a very successful Entrepreneur. Even in the midst of his worst financial situation, he personally was on the hook for over $90,000,000, he was determined to never lose his focus. Today, according to Forbes magazine he is worth well over 2.7 billion dollars, yes that billion with a 'B' . Meaning that in a rather short period of time, during one of our worst 'recessions' ever, Trump found a way to grow his net worth by over 3.5 Billion dollars. Therefore to paraphrase an old ad , "when he talks, I listen."

Recently I was listening to an audio version of his book." *Think big and Kick Ass*," he devoted an interesting section on something that I have always considered to be of vital importance, and now that I see that he considers **Focus** to be just as important, I think this is a good place to address the idea.

In an interesting twist of pop culture integrating itself into the business world, many folks still hear Mr. Miyagi saying "Focus Daniel-san" when the subject is addressed. But even using that reference we can see that with the proper application of focus and concentration we can accomplish almost anything. Even if a fly swatter would have been easier.

However, I'd like to address the idea of focus from something of a 'reverse' angle and tell you that yes you do need to keep your focus on your business, but it's the unassuming 'distractions' that can be the most dangerous. For example, if you're a man, one of the oldest and most treacherous distractions is in your female companionship. Now before the ladies string me up, let me say that this is a two way street, but men fall prey to this easier than women.

How often do we read in the sports section the story of a top seated athlete losing his ranking, possibly his whole title, shortly after he gets married or changes female companions? Take Golf for example, Tiger Woods came from almost obscurity into a master's jacket virtually overnight. He meets a supermodel, starts a family, and in one more night he's not only no longer leading the pack, in many instances he's not even competing.

Understand, I commend him for stepping back and raising a family, and making the time to treat everyone well. However if he had said from the beginning, "Guys I'm taking some time off to be a dad," I think the world would have applauded his decision. The chances are that as a newly minted "family man he probably could have kept up his sponsorships, thus his lifestyle. But we all know now, why he never came out and made that statement, because of course that's not what he was doing. This of course was made worse when it all became public, not only was he not focusing on his family he wasn't even trying to support that ideal in any form.

Maybe Golf's not your game, perhaps the example could be made with Andre Agassi and Brooke Shields, apparently in their situation she wanted to start a family and in an effort to acquiesce he stepped out of the tournaments for a few years. Or if sports don't do it for you, look at entertainers Nick Lachey and Jessica Simpson, they went on TV their careers reversed in popularity and then she lost focus, this time, on the very relationship that made her popular. So you can lose your focus in either direction.

But for the entrepreneur the focus that your going to have to rely on is the focus to maintain your course in building your business, regardless of what's going on around you. The previous examples are exactly why I make sure that my partner is on the same level I am when it comes to developing our business. Maybe your partner doesn't have the skill set to take an active part in your business, can they do everything else you need done in order for you to maintain your focus on your business? Before you start any endeavor make sure that you and you partner are on the same page when it comes to your business.

So, you and your partner have come to an agreement, they are willing to take on a little more of the load at home, so that you can focus on your business, what else is there that could divert your gaze from your business? Unfortunately almost everything that distracts you during the day, could cause you to lose your focus on your business. I worked with a gentleman one time on a project that he was very excited about, during the pre launch phase he found an area of the internet where he could promote his business and "discuss" the ins and outs with other entrepreneurs. Unfortunately what ended up happening was that this area turned out to be 'controlled' by several folks who basically asserted themselves as 'bullies' and spent the majority of their time doing their best to discourage other folks from not running their businesses, but from even spending any time involved in their business. I don't quite understand the whole mindset, but I guess the thought was that if they could convince you to spend your productive time engaging them then you couldn't be running your business very effectively?

Unfortunately that's exactly what happened. This gentleman spent so many hours, morning and evening, sparring with them on the internet, that he never applied any of his talents to this business and it finally just fell by the way side. By then of course, his partner, who had been made many promises, was so frustrated at not having a husband and now not having a business, she just lit into him. Unfortunately many people confuse **activity** with **productivity** and because they feel they are busy, they assume that they must be making progress.

Finally of course the business itself may have a number of 'land mines' full of attention getters that will pull your focus completely off your intended business. For example, I attended a business seminar recently which was aimed at entrepreneurs looking to expand their marketing efforts through several programs that the speaker had designed. Not ever wanting to reach the point where I feel I know everything about any subject I thought that this should be a worthwhile seminar to attend.

When the speaker took the platform he started to explain that his marketing programs were so effective that you were going to need to be prepared to be able to handle the added income properly. OK, I've been in business long enough, he was trying to "spin the dream", so as to validate the money that he would no doubt, ask you to invest in his program when it was all said and done. But once he had you all set to spend the extra income you were about to enjoy, the very next presenter got up and started talking about tax attorneys, and running afoul of the law, and trust accounts in your grand kids names and he actually said "if your in business you will run afoul of the IRS." Now I'm not sure how everyone in the room thought, but I do know that from that statement forward, no one sitting around me, heard another single word that came from this presenters mouth. As a matter of fact one couple actually got up and walked out saying "well we obviously can't afford to get into this kind of business."

Even if we ignore the fact that this seminar had in effect, changed several folks concentration from making a sale, to not making a sale. It even seemed to have the effect, by just mentioning a possible IRS involvement, in taking someone's focus off of their own business and instead focusing it on the upcoming issue, that doesn't exist. Now I'm not saying that you wont ever have an IRS problem, according to their own web sites one out of every 3 million folks in America will be called into their office for a conversation at some point or another. But to start someone who believes that they are doing the right thing day in and day out, thinking that the appointment will definitely be on its way, is just a down right scare tactic. What's worse, this particular presenters use of this tactic not only effected his sales, but those of everyone after him.

Now, I don't know what kind of business that this couple ran, but lets say that they owned a small print shop. Now you have, at least ½ of the managing partners so worried about a visit from the IRS that they may now return to their office and start going over their paperwork with a fine toothed comb. To make sure that the papers are "in order" for the IRS audit, which may never come. There are many differing opinions as to why you are in business, but really the bottom line for why most folks are in business for themselves is to generate an income such that their business can grow at a comfortable rate. As well as grow at a rate that will leave them enough profit to continue to expand their retirement options. I don't want to pay the IRS anymore than I have to, but I am certainly not going to lose my forward focus just on someone else's ideas.

We have looked at the personal and we have examined some of the business reasons why you may lose focus, but the most insidious reason, the absolute worst way to lose your focus, is something that you as the entrepreneur do, or don't do. This is caused by one of the things that you can stand diligent watch over every single day, yet through one small mistake, it could all grind to a halt. That mistake, that one item that you should guard yourself against above all is so prevalent, yet such a "small thing" that many will laugh at its mention, but I will predict that above anything else, this could bring your business to its knees. Please don't think that I'm trying to be catty by drawing this out, neither am I trying to frighten you out of your business. I do, however, want you to understand the importance of this item.

What is it that you should guard against? How can you prepare yourself? What can you do, to make sure that you, as a business owner, don't get **bored**. Yes boredom, leads to the loss of focus and interest, it leads to the easy lure of a paycheck from someone else, more than anything else. One day, you will be looking through the bills, and it will hit you, 'wow this just isn't any fun anymore', that's when you know it has started, and that's what you want to watch for.

Suddenly so many things that you do will seem so mundane and meaningless. You may start to get 'agitated' at the number of returns you are processing one month, or the electric bill comes in a little bit higher than you expected, and you start remembering the days when those were someone else's responsibility. You start to think about those months where your paycheck was a certain amount and you knew how much that would be, and when it would be in the bank. You realize that it was nice to be able to go to the bank and them not know who you are, because you have an outstanding note for several hundred thousand dollars.

What do you do to combat boredom? You do the same things that you did to get yourself into business in the first place. You remember those pay checks coming in through an ACH, and you remember how depressing it was to realize that the 60" plasma you saw on sale, would have to wait, again. You think back to the times when a big treat was going out to Golden Corral to eat, you and your sweetie, and you both really enjoyed it, but even then you seemed to always share a dessert, not because it was romantic, but because you would need gas on the way home. You remember the many times when you got up on Monday and you had zero stress, because you knew what you were going to do when you got to work that day, and the next and the next, and then you started to realize that entire seasons would pass without any surprises, and how you dared not use the "b" word because you knew, as soon as you did, something would break and administration would then be breathing down your neck for the next 27 hours.

So how do you keep from getting bored? How do you combat stress? Two ways really, I'll let you choose: First you can run your business on such a string and a prayer that every day is full of excitement and every night is full of wonder on how you got through the day. You remember that yes it may have felt nice for someone else to be the scapegoat, it was even nicer to know that if today you want it to be 'hat day' then today is 'hat day.' You realize that although there are six other businesses you could go into, the one that you have chosen is the best vehicle for your future.

The other alternative, and the one that I choose, is to look at the business your in a fresh way every day. To understand that no matter how successful your business seems to be now, that its on 'auto pilot' and there are more and better ways to extract money from the world. You know that by just looking at your business on a slightly different level you can find some new and exciting way to generate more business. Better yet, by just looking at it from a slightly different angle you can find entirely new markets to open up, new markets that you can explore at your pace, at your leisure and knowing that the results and the profits will be entirely yours to explore. You know that just by staying focused on your business, and letting everyone else focus on theirs, you can create something that may take care of you and your family, for life.

See, whether it's stress or boredom, the solution is the same, either accept your fate as the 'way things are', or look at your business and your customers in a brand new way everyday. Look at them, as though they are all on vacation, how could you sell to them? Watch them as though they were all retired and on a fixed income, what can you offer them? See them as though each one was independently wealthy and walked around with $5,000 in cash in their pocket everyday, how can you get your share? The choice is yours, which do YOU choose?

Jerome L. Hess

9. Preparing for Launch day

So far I haven't been able to tell you anything that will dissuade you from becoming an entrepreneur? This is a good thing, however there are a few things that you should consider before you reach your business launch day. A few of these things you will do to help prepare you for launch and some of these things you will want to do because you may not have time to do them for a very long time.

What kind of things are we talking about? Well how about items like this:

1) **Check your emotions at the door:** Starting and owning your own business is not for the sensitive or weak hearted. The information that I've given you so far isn't actually designed to scare you, just to give you a taste of what's waiting for you, once you do get started. But some folks do find it very frightening and a little unsettling. Therefore you want to find a way to keep your emotion's protected and under wraps. Once the folks who are in a business anything like the one you want to open find out that you wear your heart on your sleeve, they start sharpening their claws. Sometimes they will be using these claws to scare you, more often they are preparing to jump on the coattails of your work and find a way to market *their* goods to *your* customers.

One of the most common terms that you will hear in business today, whether its in your company or someone else's, is "comfort zone." This term can mean almost anything, but typically it's a term used to describe the "feelings" that someone has when they are nice and warm and comfortable, usually just after a Sunday chicken dinner. Unfortunately that kind of nice warm fuzzy typically only comes at grandma's house after a Sunday dinner. They certainly don't belong in business, but finding a way for the average person to be able to separate themselves from those feelings is the challenge. This is business, and on the bottom line no one really cares about your warm fuzzies. However in the same idea you need to understand that the days of bloodless, cut throat, unfeeling business owners are certainly a bygone error of the 1980's.

OK, now I understand that it just feels like I just contradicted myself right? Not exactly, here's what were talking about . The business owners who come up with one idea for business and then pursue it to the bitter end, regardless of the consequences. All the while losing friends, family and financial resources means that you have found a business owner who has fallen in love with their business or product. This is not always a bad thing except in the case where they want to remain wed to it through the bitter end. Having persistence and the willingness to stick through it to the very end is a great asset. However, most folks don't understand that in America alone it took a certain manufacturing giant over 20 years to sell the idea of personal deodorant to the American public. Folks are resistant to change, and sometimes you have to understand when your product or business is just not going to sell. You have to be able to determine when that may happen and if so, when you need to cut your losses. Unless you and your company are solvent enough to weather through however many years, or decades, it will take for the idea to catch on. Unfortunately some ideas never catch on, and some that should, are deliberately 'stifled' by other companies while other issues are worked out in the background.

The bottom line is, the first time the thought crosses your mind that sounds something like ," Well I don't care if it has termites, I love that house." You have crossed the line and need to be reeled back in. The statement I use is the same whether I'm buying a house, or a car or something as small as a laptop, "Don't get emotionally involved in the project, until three days after you have paid for the item.

2) Schedule time now for personal events: You had a life before you became an entrepreneur. You need to have a life now that you have become an entrepreneur. One of the things you do not want to do is sacrifice your family relationships on the alter of business building. The best way to make your family feel special, without actually having them involved in your business, is to setup personal time with your family as far in advance as you can.

Everyone understands that you're not a mind reader, and emergencies will arise, but there are certain things that you can plan on. Christmas generally falls on the same day every year, although my family determined early on that holidays happened whenever everyone was present. Barring Mom's birthday, most things were "moveable feasts." Of course this followed the idea that if 'Momma aint happy, aint nobody happy." But not everyone is that flexible. Typically if you will sit down and spend an hour every six months planning out your schedule, both long and short term, you will find more peace at home, and your family will be much more supportive of the time you are investing.

Let's take just a minute and go over some of the basics of that kind of planning. First of all, understand that as an entrepreneur this should not be your first session of goal planning. If it is please check out Remote Control Manager or Remote Control Professional, each has a great chapter on goal setting laid out from several different viewpoints. But essentially you need to have a calendar or calendars for the next 6 months and then some long term calendars spreading out for the next 5 to 10 years. I know this seems rather extreme, but it will pay off in the end.

Before you sit down for your planning hour gather up a few items, 1st get your anniversary book or whatever you currently use as your datebook, make sure you have your families birthdays anniversaries and any other important dates (graduations, contests, etc.), then lock yourself in a room alone, turn off the phones and start laying everything out. Do not leave out anything, your birthday, anniversaries, graduations, Christmas, it doesn't matter how obvious things look, write them down. Entrepreneur is Greek for "work your tail off', you will not have the chance in 3 weeks to stop and scribble in some things that you forgot, so write everything down. When your done you may even want to ask your personal partner (not your business partner) to look over what you have to see if you left anything out. Remember little Johnny's Pinewood Derby race 'can' be attended by Mom, but wouldn't Dad rather be there?

Try as you might, you will forget some things, your only human, something will be forgotten or something unexpected will arise, you want to try and cover everything you can in advance. Additionally 'family' things will come up, Bob get's married Mary get's pregnant, there are dozens of things that can happen, prepare yourself in anyway that you can.

The bottom line is this, you will spend more time than you want, earn less than you expect, and work harder than you ever have in your life. You deserve to have the chance to relax and enjoy whatever the event or holiday is, even if you're smart enough to just decide you want a day off to recharge your own batteries. By planning those out in advance you have every right to turn off your cell phone and ignore the knock on the door. Make sure you schedule that in advance.

3) **Plan to give business to others:** OK, now you are sure that I have just lost my mind, right? Wrong, I'm not talking about giving your business to others, but if you will carry around a very few select business cards, the way I'm going to outline for you, you will engender more goodwill and increase your referral rate easier than any other way.

For example, if your opening a Fiat repair shop, and someone brings you a brand new Porsche Cayenne that has that "funny noise", and your not comfortable with working on German automobiles, then make sure that you have on hand the name and number, preferably a business card, for the best Porsche repair shop that you can find. Now I understand that its almost impossible to meet and greet everyone who is in a similar business as yours. But chances are good that you have probably had the opportunity to get to know folks in your area in ancillary businesses, if they are someone that you would refer your mom to, get their business card. I have been going to the same mechanic for almost 30 years and over 9 cars. I keep coming back for two reasons, first I'm very hard on cars, next he will actually, and has in the past, told me when something is not worth fixing. He could have charged me $1500 for a major repair, and instead just said, well we can fix this, but within 6 months you're going to have to fix that and that and these and... That's the kind of guy I want helping my mom. I have probably referred over 1000 people to him over the years.

Next, if someone comes to you with a great piece of business, one that you could make a tremendous amount of profit on, but you're not really sure that you can provide the customer with great follow up and follow through, find someone else to either give the business to or at the very least share the business with. In the end you will have more business and more long term success if you bring great customer service along with someone else, than if you provide, fair service or fair products to customers who are moderately happy.

Be generous with your referrals, when appropriate, and you will find that your customers are happier, that they are served more fully, and will return to you over and over again. They will refer their friends and family to you, and you will serve them time and time again, these are the things that will keep you in business, keep you sane and keep your family happy.

10. Propositions for your Business

No these aren't those kind of propositions, or are they? There are basically 5 format questions that you want to keep in mind when you present your business or any part of it. The good news is that once you figure these things out they can become second nature, the bad news is that they can never afford to become static or boring. To keep things simple I call it "My 5 U's" and I know that some smart aleck will point out that its 4 U's and an I, but you know that just does not roll as well. Nor does it really work as a memory jogger.

As you develop these you will find that you are constantly working and reworking them, and that's a good thing. However there are two dangers that you do want to watch for, the first is in *overworking* a concept and the second is in *not working enough* to really hone in on what it is that makes these a good fit for your business. In almost everything else in your business there comes a time when you have to say "good enough is good enough" and submit what you have. In the case of your 5 propositions you really want to continue working on these until they become such a natural extension of your business that they become an automatic response to certain questions.

Why are these so important? As mentioned earlier, these will become responses to almost any question about your business, therefore a perfect fit is required. Some folks look at them as though they are an extension of their "elevator speech," which is not a bad analogy. But an elevator speech can change depending on who you are talking to, your propositions should remain the same unless something about the core of your business changes. You will use them in marketing and advertising, when giving public and private presentations about your business. They will become so second nature that if woken from a dead sleep and asked for one of the 5 they will be the only response that comes to mind.

5 Unique Propositions:

1) USP – Unique Selling Proposition

Although we have touched on this one a bit lets go back and explore it a little more, as it really is that important. The USP should answer the one question all customers have in mind when they first hear about you and your business: **Why should I choose to spend my hard earned money with you as opposed to any other option?** Now I'm sure that as you read this dozens of different ideas are running through your head, but let me point out a few challenges that you must keep in mind when developing your answer.

Now one of the ideas that may be coming to mind, that shouldn't is something like, "But my prices are so much better than the competitions." You want to stay away from this for so many reasons, but the bottom line is that this is one fight you can't win. There is always one choice that is cheaper than any price you can put on your product. How do I know this? Because there is always the option for the customer to not buy anything at all, and save all the money and the time and the effort.

Now I know that you don't really think that not buying is a valid choice that you have to compete against, but it absolutely is, it's always out there. In fact in some personality types it is almost the default decision that they will come to if left to their own devices.

As you develop your business and start to develop more of your events and products your going to find that you will need one USP that is a continuing and ongoing USP for your business. Then you will have several smaller, minor ones that are specifically in support of specific products or events that are generated from your company. A good example of using a USP is from a client of mine who runs a training company and his USP involves developing 'rapport' with your clients. He has it in his logo, on his masthead, on every piece of literature and page of his website.

Now that seems pretty obvious, but watch how you take this a step beyond the obvious. Taking that central USP he has now written a book on how to develop rapport with your customers. But wait it doesn't stop there, because then he found a certification course that he could become a Master Trainer of, allowing him to develop an entire course or boot camp around.. Having information like this allows you to become a 'certified expert' in "gaining rapport." There is more, he has an entire series of presentations that he has developed, ranging from 5 minutes to 90 minutes, all revolving around his USP and all demonstrating how rapport, once integrated into your business or employees, can expand your volume, your referrals and positively effect your bottom line. Not everyone will find a single USP that can be manipulated into so many different aspects and product lines of their business, but what if you could? How much could that add to your bottom line?

2) UVP - Unique Value Proposition

Much like the USP the Unique Value Proposition is a statement that you will generate and use about your product or service that will answer this question in your customers mind: "Your product is not the cheapest, but why is it a better *value* than everyone else's?" Once you address that question you will find that you have been freed up from trying to compete head to head in the pricing wars.

As we mentioned earlier, there should be no real "competition" in your field once your product or service gets thrown into the mix. Your UVP is your chance to prove it. After all the open market is like one big state of Missouri, "SHOW ME." In other words, don't just tell me that your product is a better value, but show me how it's a better value. Understanding of course that 'better value' does *not* mean 'lower priced.' Point in fact I can demonstrate several options that you currently have to buy a steak in your area. For example there is a grocery store somewhere near you, like my town they probably charge anywhere between $2 and $5 a pound depending on what cut of steak you want. Also, if you look towards the slightly 'better' neighborhoods in your area you may be lucky enough to find a butcher, although they aren't as plentiful as they once were, they are still out there, and they are probably priced between $3 and $7 per pound. Finally, even if you live in the wilds of Alaska and have Phone or Internet service there is a certain Steak company in the 'windy city' that will overnight your steak to you, at a cost of $30 per pound, not including shipping.

Now I typically find that there are two very important parts of the UVP that most folks leave out when they develop what they feel is "the one" for their business, first are the intangibles and next is the concept of 'stacking.' I'll go over these one at a time here, but you really want to plug into our Entrepreneur Institute for a very insightful afternoon of detailed development.

First of all the intangibles are typically missed or sometimes 'glossed over' by business owners because they find that they are so difficult to put into words. They may have identified and even named the absolute icon for their ideal customer, but if they don't relate to that person very well they are going to have a tough time 'speaking their language.' Every generation has their own vocabulary and inside each generation every sub-culture has it's own vocabulary. If you're a 40 year old business owner trying to sell a "Rock and Roll" lifestyle to college students, you are going to end up very broke and rather foolish looking.

But consider this, if you want me to come eat at your restaurant, you can tell me all day long that I will in fact save money by eating at your restaurant, but if that's the only thing you are trying to appeal to, you will have a very empty diner. I love seeing restaurants with signs outside "Just like Momma used to make." What if your mom was a lousy cook? Admittedly, they are trying to market to the intangible but surely there is a better way to do it. Let's go back to the restaurant, if yours is not a 5 star fine dining restaurant, but instead you have the naugahyde booths and the red check table cloths and lots of comfort food, what are your positive intangibles you can market to? Run a special any day but Mother's day and say "Mom has been working all day, just like you have, doesn't she deserve a break? Bring her and the kids down to Momma Leone's for some great home cooked comfort food with the tender Roast Beef you love, the calorie counting Chicken she craves and the Hamburgers and Hot Dogs that your kids are asking for, best of all, we clean up the mess."

You have just stacked intangible on intangible and appealed to mom and dad both, while giving dad the chance to appear the hero. This could be a Radio or TV spot just as easily as a print or billboard ad, better yet a direct mail piece. You have also just been introduced to 'value stacking,' but in a slightly more rudimentary method. Value stacking is the idea that the individual values of each item in your "deal" , when added together, will add up to so much more than the pittance that you're asking for the whole bundle makes this such a bargain. Again you are giving the customer so much value for what they are giving to you that they would have to be from off planet not to take advantage of your sale.

For example in the case of the family style restaurant, you have already stacked the intangibles, look like a hero, give mom a break, everyone gets what they want, we clean up, so now lets stack the tangibles. Most restaurants do this with their "value meals", but since you don't serve 'paper ware' your approach could be in the expense of trying to cook 3 or 4 separate meals so that everyone gets what they want, in conjunction with the drinks etc. This idea, allows you to stack value upon value upon value. In other types of businesses the perceived value is actually something that can be inflated at almost every angle. Instead of a restaurant maybe you sell Credit Card Machines? Add on the value of an $80/hour installation, better yet, throw in the value of your 24 hour tech support line, once you include the cost of lifetime free upgrades, the value gets higher and higher and higher in the eyes of the customer, while your cost goes up little if any.

3) UEP - Unique Experience Proposition

The Unique experience proposition is often not used in smaller businesses because the owners feel that this is tied directly to status, but nothing could be farther from the truth. Many of the best UEP's I have seen have almost been in reverse from the norm.

Ask yourself this, what makes eating at your restaurant, shopping at your store or dropping my car off with your mechanic, different than the restaurant, retail store or repair shop, down the street? Especially if I am paying more for the opportunity, what about the experience is so unique? I know some mechanics have a valet service to and from your job. Some offer to arrange a car rental. What can you do that's different, that doesn't need to eat at your profit?

Now this can be flexible dependent upon your particular type of business, but in the end it all revolves around your 'ideal' customers opinion of what the entire experience was, after all is said in done. The good news for you is that even though some of the specific details may fluctuate dependent upon your business, the ideas that you use don't have to change. Remember, as much as you want to say, " That won't work in my town (state, business, this economy, etc.), you're not allowed to say those things anymore. We can demonstrate without the shadow of a doubt, that what works for A works for Q, and if folks is Florida like it, folks in Ohio will as well.

How does that work? Well lets go through several examples and develop them for the customers and see how we can effect their experience.

Let's look at our restaurant owner and see what we can do to modify the experience her diners may have. Now from interviewing our Entrepreneur over a period of months we determined that her ideal customer is defined as "Tim." Tim is 34 years old, he has a white collar job, and he has at least a 4 year college degree, Tim is single, but looking, but because of the area that this restaurant is in, Tim is also living an 'alternate' lifestyle. The area that the restaurant is in is within 2 miles of the condo that Tim bought 3 – 5 years ago, it faces the water and is not on the first floor. Once Tim gets off work, in season, he puts on his tank top and shorts and pulls his 10 speed down to the boardwalk and begins a 5 mile ride.

Tim says that the ride is for exercise, yet with all the conversation stops and the dinner followed by drinks he usually comes back with more calories than when he left. Tim owns a car, but prefers the outdoors, so he walks or rides his bike to most events. He loves the free Jazz concerts that the city hosts every Sunday afternoon and the volleyball games on Saturday. Often Tim will come in for lunch by himself, but if he comes in for dinner he almost always has someone with him.

So how can we make Tim's time off the kind of experience that he will integrate as part of his ride every day of every weekend? To start with, we need to take at least 2 full parking spaces at the front door that are not handicap, and turn them into Bike/Scooter parking. If you can specify motorcycles in another slot that's great, but the 1st two up front are bicycle or scooters only. Additionally, the chances are very good that if Tim works in a white collar career, he's probably also on line, therefore open up your router and offer 'free WIFI with purchase" it could be a coke, but he needs to buy something. Plus you will find that if your drinks (even non alcoholic ones) are good enough they will want to keep ordering. Also, make sure there are enough outlets near your tables/booths. There is nothing sadder than the 10 foot sign that says free wi fi, only to have 2 folks having stare downs for the one AC outlet in the entire dining room. If that's going to create an expense, maybe a 'recharge station' someplace secure, could serve a similar purpose.

Additionally, since Tim will be alone at lunch you should have 2 specials every lunch, one very light and calorically friendly, and the other one a GLUT. Some days he will want to remain active and some days he will just want to feed his hunger. Alternatively at night you will do better serving many appeteazers, smaller seemingly lighter finger foods that are low cost and low effort for the restaurant, but express a higher perceived value to the customer. Also hosting 'events' on a regular basis can not only attract groups but open up your potential crowd as well. Although Tim is the ideal client, letting your local Toastmasters or Science Fiction Book Club know that you have a room that they can use, that has WiFi, can become very appealing to a variety of different folks.

In summary, Tim will occasionally be looking to satisfy his hunger, but if you can provide him with a unique and seemingly individualized experience that is almost tailored to his needs, you will build a repeat and referral customer base that will maintain your bottom line throughout every season.

But, what if you don't ever see your customer? If your in B2B or a web hosted business, or even just in remote coaching, how can you make sure that the experience that your customer has is one that is unique to you and yet will maintain the appearance of being not only too inexpensive to pass up, but too costly to duplicate. In case one of the other businesses in town decides to "shadow shop" your company?

Interestingly enough I have a client who runs a 'coaching/consulting' business for parents of talented teens looking to leverage those talents the best they can to offset college expenses. What can she do to make her customers experience not only unique, but appear as to have a value far in excess of the small investment they pay her ?

In her situation her ideal customers are the 'Joneses.' Mr. and Mrs. Jones have been married 20 years have 2 children, one in High School one is Middle School, one pet and they have lived in their home more than 5 years and have a combined income of about $75,000 a year. Also, at least one if not both children have expressed a tremendous affinity for an after school program, and they want to use those talents to see how many scholarships, grants and other opportunities there are available to assist them. Unfortunately due to several unexpected events the college fund that Mr. and Mrs. Jones started 16 years ago, has been neglected almost to the point of being non existent. How can their experience be unique and positive?

For privacy's sake we will call this owner Kelly, and explain that she learned everything she knows about this by putting her 3 kids through the path that she promotes. Right off the bat one of the unique things that sets Kelly apart is that she offers a free 15 minute telephone consultation with anyone who is considering becoming a client. Although this is not a requirement it is a strongly encouraged option that is available. Kelly has found that the clients she can talk to before they start up, will give her additional information about their particular situation that can help her, customize their experience. Also Kelly can take that 15 minutes to promote her program, her confidence in getting the Jones children the assistance they need. While also allowing Kelly the chance to explain how booking space for the Jones's other child now, will help keep expenses down.

Next Kelly has 3 levels of activity within her training program, the first involves a 200 page paperback book that Kelly wrote, outlining her ideas and using her own experiences as examples throughout. The cost of the book is slightly higher than average, but she has not only published it in a 'Trade Paperback format, thus increasing perceived value, but has packed it full of information. All but the most astute readers will find themselves wanting more when they are done reading it, which she is prepared to deliver in spades.

Everyone who purchases her book is automatically signed up for a 90 day subscription to her Level 1 coaching program. Level 1 does many things, some of the highlights of which are: A Bonus CD arrives 14 days after their book ships, on the CD are samples and examples of applications, letters of recommendation and some of the names and addresses of administrators of the colleges in the new client's area. Two weeks after they receive the CD they will find a "Newsletter" in their mail box stocked with 4 – 8 pages of information, interviews with parents who have followed her system, interviews with Administrators at colleges, and a time and date for so that they may call in for 1 hour of coachingl. Part of the coaching program includes telephone coaching, so Kelly wants to get their feet wet, by allowing them to "listen in" on her regular coaching calls.

Two weeks after they receive the newsletter they get their next Bonus CD, which is a recording of her Level 2 coaching call. Again this arrives un announced and in a very large padded envelope with the words "Un Announced BONUS" written on the outside. Interestingly enough, if one were to hold them closely enough they might actually find that the new CD that arrived is the audio version of one of the articles in the previous Newsletter they received. Recycling is good, recycling information is better.

Finally, just before she receives her second newsletter/bonus CD or even the special Feature DVD that I know Kelly is working on, Mr. and Mrs. Jones will receive an email, a letter via US Mail and if provided, a phone call, inviting them to be part of the special insiders group who are being offered a unique price on the Advanced level of coaching. This of course can only be offered to a limited number of folks since it includes one on one coaching as well as group coaching for one year, or more. Guiding them through the maze of paper work that they will encounter between 9th grade and College Graduation.

It's my firm belief that with all the bonuses and extras and special events that are being offered to the customer, above and beyond what they expect, how could they not be impressed. Now I have seen some clients tell me that a UEP is just too expensive. I suggest we do some very simple math and break it down to see just how expensive this might be.

Starting with Kelly's costs:

Book Printing:	$2.50
Delivery:	$2.00
Bonus CD:	$ .35
Delivery:	$2.00
Newsletter:	$1.00
Delivery:	$2.00
Conf Call:	$3.00/person
Bonus CD:	$ .35
Delivery:	$2.00
Newsletter:	$1.00
Delivery:	$2.00
Bonus CD:	$ .35
Delivery:	$2.00
Newsletter:	$1.00
Delivery:	$2.00
Total Invested:	$23.55

Customer Orders Book for $25 + 4.95 s/h

Total Profit in first 90 days $6.40

You may not think your ready to retire yet, but now the payment for the next months coaching kicks in, for Kelly this means no less than $24.95, for Level 1 and if they chose to upgrade to Level 2 or 3 could be as much as $97.97 a month.

I know, because I helped establish her pricing guidelines. These were created when Kelly first established her business and she had 27 folks pre-order her book. Of the 27 pre orders, remember the book hadn't even been written at that point, when asked if they felt that on going contact and support from the author would be helpful all 27 responded affirmatively. When asked about methods of contact that would best suit them 12 responded 'in writing', 10 wanted to speak with her and 7 felt that having a website of information would fulfill their needs.

Looking at the way Kelly has her business structured, these 27 folks could actually break down to 12 level 1 members at $24.95 a month, 7 level 2 members at $47.93 a month and 10 level 3 members who could be generating no less than $97.97 a month. Making the math simple we are looking at Level 1 memberships of $299.40 per month, Level 2 memberships generating $335.51 a month and Level 3 members adding $979.70 per month. This looks interesting, but we are talking business, and remember we are giving away the first 3 months, but that means that annually these 27 pre orders could generate almost $15,000 per year, of course the second year would be slightly higher since it would generate income all 12 months.

What did Kelly do? She determined who her ideal customers were, what they looked like, and what they specifically needed in order to make them feel most comfortable with using her program to get their kids into the college of their choice. Not only did she give them what they needed in the best manner that they could understand, but she allowed the customer to "call the shots," and in return they will maintain their memberships with her business for as long as they feel she is generating a value for them. Again, the figures here are all based strictly on supposition, if I told you that the reality was actually much, much higher, I would be telling you the truth. Kelly is a very good business person and she is very good at relating to her customers. Many of the couples will drop out after their first child gets into college, but since we maintain electronic databases of all customers, we know when their next child enters high school and can then send them a reminder that if they have any questions or challenges they know where to turn for help and answers.

In some cases building a "positive" **UEP** seems like an almost insurmountable task, and there's nothing wrong with admitting that. If you own a business that doesn't lend itself in any way, shape or form, to a "positive" experience, than what you need to do is make sure your customer knows that there is no where else in the world (or at least in your town) where they can do business with someone who is better equipped to solve a negative problem, than you. In this case youre not so much providing a Positive Experience Proposition, as many people believe is required, but instead you are helping your customers avoid a dramatically *negative experience,* that no one would ever want to be have happen. Imagine that you are the Entrepreneur who owns a Septic Cleaning service, building a positive experience may seem rather difficult. However building an absolute negative experience, one that is so bad that the customer will pay almost any cost to avoid, could be exactly what your business needs.

Picture this your eldest daughter has decided to get married and after 30 years she feels that hosting the ceremony on the back lawn with its sloping hillside would make the perfect backdrop. Your princess is dressed in her virginal white multi thousand dollar dress, just waiting for the moment when the music begins, and someone 'smells' something unusual. Thinking Uncle Harry ate too many cocktail wieners everyone ignores it until a blood curdling shriek is heard down the hill and halfway across the neighborhood. Immediately everyone runs towards the house, only to find the cause when they spot the bride standing in the doorway in tears her dress, suddenly wet and "discolored" from the knees down. In an effort to keep things from getting too far out of hand, no one pays too much attention to the fact that the smell seems to be getting stronger, until one of the kids mentions that the grass is wet...

Do you think we have painted a unique enough experience to avoid here? Yeah I think so to, so lets look on the other side. You happen to own the oldest hotel in 16 counties, and although it may be cooler in the winter and warmer in the summer than the guests would like, what would their opinion be of a scene that went something the following. The bride is attended by 6 bridesmaids in her own 'pre bridal' suite, which actually is a suite, not just a large bathroom, with its own sitting area where she can look out of the balcony and see the guests arrive. The groom and his groomsmen are gathered in the "library", which although containing hundreds upon hundreds of actually hard bound volumes is also a small lounge with over stuffed seating for 12 and their own personal drink attendant. The gentleman are not only supplied with the beverages of their choice but also the 'diversions' needed, cigars, appetizers, the like, Switch to the grand ballroom where the string quartet is playing stylized versions of "their song", and each guest is seated in large comfortable chairs, no 'fold a ways' here. Cut back to the brides father who hands a small white envelope to a tuxedoed staff member as he comments to his friend that having a "one stop shopping experience" allowed everyone from the bride on down to know that they only needed to contact one person, at one phone number to adjust, confirm or change anything or everything about the event.

Again, building the event, to match the business and to exceed the customer's expectations.

4) USfP - Unique Safety Proposition
One of the 'scariest' things that most business owners find in their day to day operation is the idea of returns. Now you're going to have them, but there are a few things that you can do up front, and a few things you should absolutely avoid, to cut

down the ratio of returns. Having a solid USfP is probably the best way, bar none.

Many business owners call the USfP by its 'old school' name of "Guarantee." That's because most business owners either are afraid to give a guarantee or they state it in such small terms that its almost impossible to see without a magnifying glass. FedEx actually had an entire ad campaign making fun of companies whose guarantees were stated so fast that they had to hire the "Fastest Talker" in the world, just to simulate it for us. But here is another way to look at it, If you can **not** in good conscience slowly and clearly offer a guarantee for your product or service than you should **not** be involved in that business. Almost every single thing sold, traded or bartered in this country can be guaranteed in some way shape or form without costing you a fortune, you just have to figure out how.

For example, lets say I want to become a Real Estate Agent, in my state you are required to attend a specific class that although not proctored by the state, is in theory, designed by the state. Following the completion of this class is the requirement of passing a state hosted exam. I live in a small town and this class is only being offered in one of three places. I can sign up at the Community College and attend 1 hour of class 1 day a week for 10 weeks, or Bobs Real Estate School offers class 2 hours a night 2 nights a week for 3 weeks, or Joes RE Express offers a weekend course with 8 hours on Saturday and 4 hours on Sunday. Because the state designs the course the content in these classes should be the same, each has the exact same book, and you will be taking the exact same test regardless of which class you take.

The College charges $200 for its class, Bob charges $300 for his class and Joe has the audacity to charge $600 for his class. If Joe calls you and asks you to help him market his class, what's your first move? Unfortunately Many folks would tell him that his price is out of line and if he doesn't cut it at least in half to match Bob, he will be out of business. Although that could be a valid approach its not the one I would choose. Instead I would tell Joe that he needs to make a guarantee that is so strong that several things happen. First that his 'competition' is so scared of competing with his guarantee that they wont even try. Next a guarantee that is so strong that I, as the customer, will have zero hesitation in paying 100% more than the closest school and $400 more than the cheapest school.

Sounds like quite a guarantee doesn't it, well it should, because it will be just one of the tools that Joe uses to pry my fingers off my wallet and allow him to dip in and remove my cold hard cash. He could use a multi pronged or 'stacked' approach in his advertising and word his ad something like this:

*If you attend **Joe's RE Express** we will not guarantee that you will pass the test, no one can, and if they say they will, they may lie about other things as well. What we will guarantee you is that you will receive an intense two day course of instruction from one of the finest Real Estate Brokers in our state. More importantly we have arranged our classes to occur on a schedule* *that 20 years of experience have shown is the simplest to arrange for you and the easiest to work around from your family. Additionally we will not be asking you to return week after week , unless you want to learn it again. Instead we will cover everything you need to pass your test in one weekend and allow you to determine what to do with the rest of your time. Whyeven bother to look at the states test schedule, if we see you on Saturday you could be testing on Wednesday. Which means that on Friday you can be out selling houses and earning huge commissions? In other courses it could take 2 to 6 months to take your state test, after you complete their class. The one thing that we have found is that the more time between your class and your test the worse your chances are for passing. But lets say that something happens, on the way to the test, and you don't do very well, as a matter of fact you are so distracted that you just plain don't pass. Well we will see you next weekend. Because we guarantee that you will have a seat in one of our classrooms until you do pass your test. That's right, instead of 2 or 3 shots a year for your test, we will allow you to test all 12 times this year if that's what its going to take. Were only satisfied when you have your license.*

Now I understand that, that could be construed as one of the cheesiest "used car" ads that you have heard, but the bottom ne is this: Your customer needs to feel comfortable ("safe") in sending you their money. They can see that you're not going to ride off in the sunset and never be seen again. Quite the contrary, it almost feels like you and Joe can become partners in the Real Estate Endeavour.

5) IE – Irresistible Offer

Now, if you want to complain that you think that this belongs under the marketing chapter, I'm OK with that. However, I think once you wrap your mind around the fact that everything in your business is going to be involved in marketing, it will be easier to see why I placed it here. The title says it all though, in this particular 'proposition' to your customer you are going to generate the "irresistible offer" for your prospective clients.

Invariably, anytime I bring this up I am asked the same two questions. First, why is this at the end? Next is why is this so important? I thought the first was rather obvious, it doesn't contain the word proposition, and thus flows better if placed at the end. For the second answer we will need to look a little closer at what an IE is and more importantly what its not.

In every training class I always have someone raise their hand and in a very bad impression of The Godfather mention an offer that your customer "no canna refuse." I laugh when I say that, but I also must point out that in a stretch it is close to the truth. We are not interested in making our customer think of old movies, cement galoshes or race horses. We are interested, however in generating the idea in our customer that what you have to offer them is such a value, from every angle, that they can not, in good conscience buy it elsewhere.

In the mid 1980's the health club boom was well under way, Olivia had gotten "Physical" and Bally stopped making pinball machines. Unfortunately the folks who really wanted to get involved in this trend, the twenty-something's, found that they were so busy buying workout gear and attending cardio classes that they didn't have time to eat well. They saw their only two choices as Whey Powder and Raw egg shakes or starvation. Then two entrepreneurs from out west decided that they could, at a profit, setup a *third* fast food option. At that time it was the Golden Arches or the Funny looking guy in the Crown. Wendy's and Long John and the rest were there, they were just too expensive. So these two gentleman opened a new idea in fast food, they served food that was lower in calories, lower in fat, and they had the audacity to actually print the nutritional information on every item they sold. To keep things in line they had fat free yogurt for desert, baked potatoes in place of French fries and they actually *sold* bottled water.

In the beginning they did great, their prices were only slightly higher than their competitions, an average meal was $5 where everyone else was $3, but the customers who liked the offering, came back over and over, with the idea in their head that they were eating healthy. Each of these new restaurants did offer drive thru's, but to get the most healthy meal, you needed to sit down and eat, so all their dining rooms were light colored and had lots of windows and skylights and even had live plants. Most of their core customers thought that this company would grow until they were on every corner.

Then, the unthinkable happened. The founder of Wendy's, at the time the most expensive fast food on the block, started doing advertisements. Here was your dad, or grandfather, standing behind the counter, telling you that his restaurant, now had healthy alternatives, baked potatoes and a full salad bar, kept fresh every hour. The one thing that Wendy's didn't do, was lower their prices. You would normally think that would have killed it right? Not even close, Wendy's had the one thing that the other guys didn't, they created an irresistible offer for the customers. It went something like this, Have a ¼ pound hamburger, fries and a coke for $4.50, or get a salad bar for $2.99 and get the drink for free. Now the difference between the drink you pay for and the drink you get free are pretty big. But since Wendy's was the first fast food restaurant to offer free refills, it didn't matter. Yes you had to get up to get it , but the staff smiled and gave you more of what you wanted. Of course they also took the opportunity to try and sell you a Frosty.

So, what can you see? A restaurant owner who had a great product at a great price, based on the hottest trend that swept the entire country, they should have had an advantage over every other restaurant anywhere within this country. What he got was an initial 'rush' of customers based on the novelty factor of being the 'new kid on the block.' Unfortunately, because they didn't have anything new, unique or special to offer their customers, once the novelty wore off, to set themselves apart in the customers mind, they had nothing, from the customer's point of view, to offer.

As someone who liked the restaurant, they had me hooked, and I understood that the difference in the long term, would make a bigger difference to me than the handful of change I might save going to one of the other places. But since they had never profiled their ideal customer, and they never declared a value statement, they didn't even have the traction to begin to create any offer, much less an incredible offer. Remember an incredible offer is not one that has bells and whistles, there's no neon, no video, an incredible offer is an offer that has so much value built into the offer itself that the customer could not afford to pass it up.

Now I have no doubt that there are many items in the background that contributed to their failure as a business. But I also know that if they had known who their ideal customer was, and if they had developed an offer to appeal to that person, they might still be around today. But that was then, this is now, everyone has HD, 3D, and multi gigabyte storage attached to absolutely everything, so how do you create an incredible offer?

Let's look at the auto repair shop down the street, like many shops he sits just off the main highway, in a building that he owns. He has been in the same neighborhood for decades, and most of his customers are repeat customers, and although he has a towing business, he rarely gets long term business from those customers. However, he has a statement on the bottom of his advertisements, billboards, service quote forms, and anywhere else that the customer is likely to look that says the following:" We will not ever install a good part on a bad car."

I know from personal experience what that means, but in case you don't go the same places I do, or maybe your mechanic doesn't offer the same kind of guarantee let me explain how it works. I had a great car a few years ago, nice sedan, comfortable, good gas mileage, no physical issues. One day the AC stopped working, I live in the south, AC is mandatory in our cars, so I drove over and dropped it off for an estimate. Normally he will call me with an estimate, but when I hadn't heard from him at lunch, I stopped by and asked his chief mechanic what the status was. His chief pulled me into the office and had me sit down and explained that due to several unusual factors about the way that this particular car was assembled my repair would cost slightly more than $1,100. Now that's more than I expected, but still within the ballpark of reasonability so I started to tell him to order the part, then he said, **but.** Three people you don't want a but from, your lawyer, your Dr. and your mechanic.

He said, "We can fix the AC for that, but you have a need for a Saperdefrabulator for your cooling system. Now in most cars that a small item that just above the oil pan, rather labor intensive, but it's available. However your particular year and model has two of them, one under the oil pan and one under the gas tank. As you may or may not know your gas tank is situated sideways here. To replace both of those would add another $745.00 to the bill." Wow almost $2000, that's a lot, so I asked what would happen if we didn't replace both of them? He explained that replacing one would strain the other, they would both stop working and potentially cause a fire. I'm not a

160

mechanic, but I understand a fire anywhere near your gas tank, is a really bad idea. The chief than said, "Just for the heck of it, I looked up your car in the Blue Book and the average value is $1,650." So its not worth fixing. He could have earned almost Two thousand dollars in fees, but instead suggested I go get another car, otherwise I would be buying another one when I had to, not when I wanted to, and that's not an enviable position.

In over 30 years of driving and owning cars, I have never found another mechanic who has ever said, "It's not worth fixing." My dad has told me that on several occasions, but never a mechanic. More than anything else, that brings me back to that particular shop over and over again. My family now goes there as do as many of my friends as I can convince. That is an offer that I can not refuse. For me, that's an offer that is absolutely Incredible.

So for you, in your business, you now have 5 different propositions to offer your customers. Do you have to offer all six? Absolutely not, but for every one that you add to the mix of your business, the more stable will be the platform that you will begin building your business upon. If you're not starting a new business and instead are looking to improve the business that you already have, you should have a starting point to build from for the future of your business

In the end what this all means is that you need to take a step back and examine each of these propositions and ask yourself, not how you can adapt what you already have, no band aids here, but instead how you can address each and every one of them. It's almost as though you will be building these propositions as independent columns of support in order to increase your business exponentially. The question you have to ask yourself is, do you try it piecemeal and "band aid" your business, hoping for an increase. Or should you instead take a step back and determine the best method to integrate them from a fresh perspective? How important is your business? Would you put a band aid on your plow horse if she was the only thing standing between you and the harvest? You'd probably call the vet.

11. Marketing

Whatever your business is, there is a huge chance that you will not use your marketing resources to their best advantage. Just for your information, marketing is not your yellow pages ad, or your newspaper ad, or even the billboard across from the train station. Marketing is what you do, every day, so that when folks have a choice between your business and someone else's, they suddenly realize that they really don't have a choice, it's you or they do without.

Chances are pretty good that at some point after you filed for your business license with the local government agency, that you got a call, or calls, from the local phone company, the local newspaper, the local billboard company, the local cable company the local...you name it company. All of them telling you that they are there to put your marketing on auto-pilot for you, and your only concern will be to service all the thousands of customers that they will be sending your way each and every day. Now the truth is that if you listen closely to what they say, if their sales guy is smart, you will learn something about marketing for your business that you need to learn immediately.

If it doesn't jump out at you, ask him or her, about all the other clients in your area that they have served. They will then pull out their 2000 page pitch book and start flipping through it. Now it should all become clear. Still no, you are awake, right? Because the one thing that you are going to find that you have in common with all of his examples is that, none of these folks are running a business like yours.

163

Oh don't get me wrong, if you have an Egyptian Tea House and Menswear store there may be another one of those somewhere in the tri-county area, but none of them are offering your unique selling proposition. You do have a well developed USP right? Hey, are you skipping chapters? I distinctly recall seeing something about USP's somewhere in the last chapter. I'm sure there was a reference, a sentence or two maybe, perhaps even a homework assignment?

OK, on the off chance that you think I am somehow speaking in Gaelic, your USP is the one thing that you do better than anyone else in your industry, that folks can not stop talking about. When you find out what that one thing is, find a way to make one sentence that captures it all. Domino's Pizza "Fresh Pizza delivered in 30 minutes or less" Doesn't say anything about it being hot, or tasty or even good, just quick! M&M's "Melts in your mouth, not on your hands", they don't mention what happens when you leave them in your jeans and mom washes them, just that they wont melt in your hands. Federal Express: "When your package absolutely, positively has to get there overnight", it may be in itty bitty little pieces, but it will get there.

Do you see what were looking for here, one statement that sums up the reason that your business is different, and better, than anything else even in your category. This reason will even justify why they would be willing to pay a little more for your product or service. After all in 1981 when I first heard of Domino's it cost $17 + tip to get that pizza. For $20 I could buy 5 of them at the grocery store, or two large with any toppings I want at Shakee's. But on a rainy Friday night or when the Bears were in the Super Bowl, I called Domino's. I told my wife the other day that a news item leading the day stated that the US mail was considering going to 3 day a week delivery. She was crushed, since I send most things 2 day or over night, I didn't see an issue. Understand that the first thing you come up with as a USP will probably not last you forever; notice Domino's doesn't mention 30 minutes anymore? Run down a few old ladies and that's bound to happen. But folks still order from them.

The biggest question you have about your marketing when you are getting started is, will you hire someone else to do it, or will you do it right the first time, and create it yourself? I am not saying that there are not some great and talented folks who currently work in advertising; I am suggesting however that in the 30 years I have owned businesses they have done their best to hide from the average entrepreneur. Most of these folks have a portfolio, in their portfolio are 3 options, good, better and best. Also known as 10%, 25% and 50% that does not refer to their commission instead that refers to how much of your yearly gross it will cost you to implement one of these options. Most Entrepreneurs have everything that they need to handle the majority of their on marketing during their first 5 years in business. They have the best understanding of what makes their business unique, they have the most invested in its success and they have an understanding of exactly who the target market for their business is, what they look like and where they live.

As a matter of fact in most entrepreneur oriented marketing courses there is an exercise that is aimed at helping you create the perfect model of exactly what your ideal customer looks like and what they do, typically they will call this customer projection your 'avatar.' If created properly your avatar will demonstrate all the way down to how often they vacation, where and with whom. But lets say that again you have a pretty specialized store, you have determined that you will be the only Egyptian based Tea Lounge and Clothing Café. What's the average age of your customer, are they male of female, are they college educated, you sell tea and clothes, which one provides the best profit margin.

Finally where does your customer spend most of their time when they are not in your store! Answer those questions and you are on your way to creating the marketing campaign of the decade. From my previous comments please don't think that I don't encourage you to get a Yellow Pages ad and a listing in the newspaper. Sometimes that's the cheapest way to become listed in the "where to" web sites. But understand that a full page ad in either the paper or the phone book is not going to give you enough room to create a desire in your customer or give them enough information on why they want to drive to your store, when they could walk to 7-11 on the corner.

This is where your USP comes in, again you have no competition, no one in your area has exactly what you have, sold exactly the way you sell it, or offers the warranty that you do. I can hear you saying now. "But J, its tea, how much of a warranty can we offer." Try this one: If you don't immediately feel like you have stepped back 600 years into the central Mediterranean region by the atmosphere in our establishment than your first onion Falafel is free! Now obviously I just made that one up, but again what is it about your store, about your staff, about your product, that makes them so special?

I was a Mortgage Broker in the mid west a while back, I was brand new in town, but I knew how to handle my business, unfortunately my wardrobe was on a truck that was 9 weeks behind me. I could not afford to stay out of work that long. So I asked around for referrals from my friends. One said "Oh JC P's has the best prices in town, and they have everything that you need right there.", meanwhile, one of the top guys in the office said "There's a little place on 13th, looks like a hole in the wall, but they will take very good care of you." Up to that point I had never bought a custom suit, they had always been gifts, so I wasn't sure what to expect, but as I'm sure you can understand the mall was, well, the mall.

However when I went to the smaller store, and it was little, the owner acted like we had been friends forever. He offered me coffee, asked me about who I liked in the ball game, and in between asked me how I found out about him, All of these answers were designed to let him know, what price range I was in, what business I was in, and what my experience was with quality men's wear. Since I was pretty new, I didn't know until later that I had spent literally twice what the mall cost me, however, I am ashamed to say that the only reason I am not

The idea is this; there was no advertising for this store. His entire marketing concept was to treat you so well that you wouldn't ever consider buying from anywhere else. When I left that town I stopped by and bought up as many items as I could afford, so that I would have some stock. When I returned 15 years later for some training on a project in a different industry, I went by and got the correct size of suit for my current frame. As you can see, to this day, over 20 years later I still tell folks about the store.

So what is it about your store, your products, your business, how you treat or service your customers, that no one else in any part of your industry can compare? Maybe you have just found out the business that you should be in, delivering that aspect of your core? Everyone has the ability to niche; most folks just don't take advantage of that ability. There was a saying once that to "Live with the classes you needed to sell to the masses? For decades that was a 100% valid statement here in America, and then Sam Walton died. Now I don't believe that everything in America that goes wrong can be blamed on Wal-Mart being the store where most people in the under $50k club shop's everyday. I will say that once he passed away and his children became involved in the business, the whole model changed. When he was alive his USP made mention of the fact that certain things were 'American Made.' Once he passed his children made their goal, ' everything in our stores is disposable.' Followed by, 'so how cheap can we sell it.' Unfortunately a large percent of America believed the advertising. Thus assuring that manufacturers would have to go to other countries, and people who wanted to sell to that class, lower their prices through the bottom of profitability and sustainability.

So how do you win the price war? Refuse to become involved in it, forget about trying to sell to the lowest common denominator and instead develop the avatar of folks that you should be selling to and find out what they want. The first person who says low price, gets a smack in the nose with the very book you're reading. Because that is just not true. I don't drink coffee, but my wife does so I have to pay for it. When I was little my mom complained about the price of coffee, but from what I can tell a pound of coffee in 1972 cost about the same as it does today. So imagine my surprise when I bought my wife a Starbucks Gift card for $50 as a stocking stuffer at Christmas only to have her tell me it was empty by Valentines Day. She has to make a special trip to go to a Starbucks. Out of curiosity I asked what the average bill at Starbucks was and she said it depended on whether she got a scone or not, but between $7 and $10. My momma woulda die.

But Starbucks has convinced their customers that they play special music, have comfy chairs, offer free WIFI (one of the first) and have turned a drive through coffee stand into a destination. The people who have the extra 30 minutes will tell you that it tastes better if you drink it there, the lower level executive types who are on their 3rd *ChocaMochaLatte El Grande* for the day would never be seen entering a meeting with a coffee cup from 7-11 or worse the vending machine. They have created a completely different perception of their product in their customers minds, to the point that people will often drive out of their way to shop with them.

If you own a restaurant, what is it that you serve better than anyone else? In the late 1980's a small bar in Clearwater Florida took the part of the chicken that no one wanted and, by dressing their waitresses differently, created an entirely new type of lunch concept, eating appetizers as a meal. Several small chains of restaurants/bars brought in clientele that would never have gone near the places, merely by selling beers that were reportedly brewed by the locals themselves. Finally, and to most men amazingly is that business known specifically as the "Day Spa." The No man's Land where women will part with hundreds if not thousands of dollars to be puffed, pampered and wrapped in seaweed. My mother who refused to get her hair wet in a swimming pool will pay extra to have another woman slather mud on her, as long as it came from the Dead Sea or a volcano located in a country she couldn't find on a map.

MUD!

It doesn't have to be fancy, just different. What do you do differently and certainly better than anyone else in your industry? Find that one thing and make sure that everyone knows about it. Find a way to link your USP with the rest of your community. For example, own a donut shop? Find out when your next PBA meeting is and bring in a few dozen. Have an Italian restaurant; you have several choices, opera, momma or the Godfather. In today's market you could actually choose any or *all* of them to develop your marketing around. One thing I will suggest, don't tie into anything too trendy. Remember the Pet Rock from the 70's? Then in the 80's it become the Punk Rock? Ok that worked, but I noticed no one wrapped it in flannel in the 90's and called it the 'slacker stone.'

Additionally, don't try and tie into anyone else's marketing campaign. Remember "Where's the beef?" it became more of a joke for Jay Leno than an ad for Wendy's at a certain point. You never know how long trends will last and you don't want to jump on the tail end of one, no matter how good it looked.

So what can you do on a limited budget to get the word out? Without registering for a $10,000 marketing boot camp let me suggest two things.

First: Create an event. Remember we talked about unusual holidays? Find four of them that you think you can wrap your concept around and go with them. They don't even have to be holidays that anyone recognizes. If you search the internet you will find one for every day of the year, and most of the time, for every item you can think of, for example: Piano Appreciation Day. Groundhog Day is very familiar, but instead of going for the animal go for a tie in with his tree stump! Better yet, find out when "Kite Flying Day" is and have a contest, The biggest the brightest the highest flying, there are more than you can imagine, so find a way to take advantage of a day. If need be create the holiday then exploit it.

Second: Target Market. Most folks will tell you that the mail is dead, and you need to start an email campaign. Well, if folks have voluntarily given you their email addresses, great, go for it, otherwise spam is worse than junk mail, it wont get opened or seen and certainly not read. However, for about $100 you can purchase a set of mailing labels of folks in your specific area, in your desired income bracket, who have a specific thing in common (like a love for Egyptian Tea). For a few hundred dollars more you can afford to mail each and everyone of these folks a personalized invitation to your specific , and very private (after all there are only 1000 folks who know about it) event. To spice up the invitation, rub some of your most pleasantly aromatic tea across the letters and promise a free bag just for coming. Be careful with how liberally you 'sprinkle' some teas look a lot like things that ought not go through the mail.

Can't do that in an email.

12. 21st Century Marketing

There are several 'tools' that have become available in the last few years that were not available to previous generations, but you need to understand how to use them. The following is just an introduction, but these are things you want to look into:

1) **Google Docs:**   They probably have a title for the whole package but there are an entire line of tools that are now available to you at little or no cost. They are being offered by the Google corporation, and there isn't any money needed from your pocket, unless you want commercial access. At this point, someone always says "But you have to give up your name," yes you do, so there is a small exchange of value. But if you register for a GMAIL account you will find that you now have access to a whole set of new tools. The best part is that these tools can be accessed by you from almost any computer almost anywhere on the planet.

From what we used to think of as a search engine has now turned into a full function portable office. From that one site with that one registration you have access to email, maps, file storage, eBooks, image storage, news, video storage, voice over IP, Blog assistance, and much more. Truly Google Docs is Google's strong entry into the world of all inclusive services for 21st century office and web integration. If Google Doc's had been available a decade ago when I was on the road 6 days a week and working in commercial banking, I could have saved myself a lot in Office Depot Fax fees.

2) Wordpress: Believe it or not there is a very valid place in this world for blogs for businesses. As a matter of fact I like that title so much I may copyright it. I will admit that I was rather confused like most folks when all these businesses, that have little or nothing to do with the internet, suddenly started publishing blogs. Then as my studies in Marketing became more intense it all started to come together. Consider this, if you should always direct your marketing **to** your customers (as opposed to **at** your customers) and you want to limit or eliminate your use of personal pronouns and self references in your advertising, where can you talk about how great you are?

Truth be told, you shouldn't, but none of us can resist telling the world how great we are, how wonderful our products and services are and how many awards we have won to prove that point. If you are going to actually avoid the entire concept of testimonials , which you shouldn't, and still want a horn blowing experience, a blog is the best place for that to happen. Where else can you take every news story, clipping and online (positive) reference to you and your company and demonstrate them for all the world to see? The blog is the perfect format.

Don't be disappointed if you have a low readership, there are ways around that, but make sure that everything that you write is there to pump you up and make your reader feel better about their choice of you and your products for the exchange of their hard earned money. You really won't find a better time and place, and no one makes it easier than Wordpress. Wordpress is free it can be very simple, and best of all, depending on the size of your organization can be written and posted by someone else. However since many of the entrepreneurs in the country like to keep things lean and mean, even if you are the Wordpress administrator, you will find, that if you can operate a web browser and a word processor (yes notepad will suffice) you can literally cut and paste your way to success.

My only two suggestions are this: First make your posting schedule something that you can live with no matter what. I cant tell you how many great blogs I have seen start as a daily post, and then move to Monday, Wednesday and Friday post, then a Monday Friday, then Friday and then, well one technology blog I have followed has their most recent post dated as October of last year. Want to lose your readers and hence your credibility? That's the fastest way.

Next, keep it entertaining. No one wants to read anything that's boring, least of all, anything that is posted on the web. You do not have to be George Carlin, but it should be relevant and entertaining. Plain and simple, if your business is to import and sell chain saws no one cares how many board feet of wood this thing can create per hour. However if your headline reads:" **The ChainSaw so Sharp even the Mutants in Texas wouldn't use it."** Well then I think you may have gone far enough out on a limb so as to get peoples attention. Again, it doesn't have to produce belly laughs, but at the first yawn kill it.(maybe even with the new Texas Massacre Reproduction model 3000).

3)Twitter/Facebook/LinkedIn – Once again, when I first saw that businesses were using these 'tools' I did not understand why or how. Even the Wall Street Journal was posting articles about "how folks will make money from social media sites", you know what they came up with? Nothing. That's right the big brains on Madison avenue teamed up with the high pockets of Wall Street and determined that someone will make money from all this, but they had no idea how. Most of these sites actually seemed to be engineered so that businesses could not make money from their presence.

Then as will typically occur, the creative, and less 'well funded', folks got involved. It is absolutely amazing what folks will come up with when their backs are against the wall and they are forced to use the tools at hand that are free. Nicely enough the companies who ruin these organizations have found ways to make money from them, but they do not yet require that you participate in this manner. Therefore you are allowed to avail yourself of all their free services, and if you plan things properly, will never need to look outside of that arena, in order to make those kinds of moves. My favorite is still the Taco stand that sent out a coupon via Twitter and instead of getting back a response of a few dozen as they intended, got back several THOUSAND and almost put themselves out of business.

Facebook and LinkedIn and now the new Google+ were all designed to allow one sort of professional or fan to connect with another. Instead they have become central breeding grounds for more commercial entities than you ever thought existed. If the

BBB tells you that in your city of 3 million people there are currently 22,743 businesses, check just your zip code on Facebook, I'll bet you will surpass that number just in your one part of your one *county*. Your challenge, as with your blog, is to keep your pages, posts and tweets entertaining, brief and of the nature that the customers will return to over and over again. There are hundreds if not thousands of books, seminars and boot camps on how best to profit from the Social sites. I don't know that any one of them is any better than the others. So as with so many things, find someone who speaks your language and learn from them. Better yet, find the pages that are sponsored by the things that you like and watch and see what they are doing, use that as a guideline for what you develop.

4) Craigslist – Most folks look at CL and see the classified ads of tomorrow, and they are pretty close. Craigslist was designed to be an open forum of trade with buyers from your local area. Personally I believe it was created in answer to how rigid and structured some of the 'other' auction sites had become. That being said there are still many ways that a smart Entrepreneur can utilize CL to its highest and best use, that of an advertising platform.

Unfortunately, straight ahead "Eat at Joe's" Style advertising is not the type of thing that craigslist is going to allow in most cases, but with a little more creativity, you can generate an entire line of ad related accessories to draw customers into your business. For example, lets say that you happen to be the proud owner of the only Flower Shop in town that has the ability to handle same day delivery. How would you utilize all the free space that Craigslist is offering? First you have to look at your business as a whole to see what else you do that no one else does. What else is it that helps set apart your business, again looking at the flower shop, you could create an entire line of hats and t-shirts that your delivery personnel could wear while making your deliveries. There are many online shirt manufacturers who will create these types of things, "on demand" ,so that you won't have to maintain an inventory, and you could sell them in your store as well as on craigslist. Additionally almost any business is available for "gift cards" what a great way to get them out and in the community of folks that will be using them, other than by using targeted advertising in those community lists on CL.

These items are only the beginning of what is available to today's marketing professional. Although IT folks have been predicting the "death of the written word" for the last 15 years, we still must consider some hard copy advertising. Point in fact there are many marketing professionals who feel that perhaps due to the number of marketers pulling out of hard copy advertising, things like direct mail and Val-pak are some of the best bargains to be had.

Add to that the flexibility and availability of the number of multimedia tools available to the marketer and you have just increased your reach by a factor of 100. A recent report published by ZDNET demonstrated that in many cases the average person is using a media sight such as youtube.com as their home page and their primary search engine. Now I find it hard to believe that most folks will ever substitute hulu.com for Google, but apparently in certain cases that's what people want, honest, accurate reviews of items they are searching for, from people just like them.

One of the most creative uses of that form of technology that I have seen in recent times involves a young lady with a restaurant in the Midwest. Her shop is in a resort town right on the boardwalk of the local "town square." In finding ways to not only get the word out about her business but also to bring attention to her, non competing , neighbors, she puts her web cam on a cart once a week and then visits a different store on the boardwalk every week. She gets to shoot a 5 minute "infomercial" about her and her restaurant as well as "interviews" her neighbors and gets them to talk about what's important to them and their friends. What do *you* think is going to be important to a business owner in a resort town with a business on that town's boardwalk? You guessed it, them, their business and their products and services. The other business owners, recognizing that they are receiving "free publicity" will always throw in comments about her store and how great it is and what excellent products she has. Anyone who doesn't, doesn't have to end up on the web site now do they? "Opps technical issue." The sheer genius behind such a "home town" low cost 'broadcast' so far surpasses everything that is being taught in today's business schools that I wouldn't be surprised to find that the manager of every Starbucks in LA suddenly appears with a web cam mounted to their head!

These are just a few of the more creative ways that folks are finding to tap into today's high tech, low cost entry to marketing. This proves once and for all that the "American" spirit is not dead, and that folks want to find vendors who share their sensibilities, and values, to take their hard earned dollars to.

Now the challenge is, how can you apply any or all of these ideas in your business, in your town? Live near Daytona or Sturgis? You have over a half a million folks coming to visit you at least once a year, and now there are rally's opening up in North Carolina, Ohio and Oregon, what will you do to leverage this sudden influx of visitors to your advantage? More importantly what can you do in advance of their arrival to encourage these visitors to seek out your business and make it a destination. Because everyone knows that in these kind of events, folks travel in crowds,

Marketing, once a necessary evil, and one you can not afford to ignore, nor can you afford to let someone else control. Unless they have a stake in your business, they will not be performing at the same high level that you will, and they will never be able to generate the excitement and the focus needed to bring in the new customers that you need to make your business a success.

13. Specifics for Service Industries

If you remember I mentioned that one of the things that make me crazy is the folks who start their sentence with "That won't work with my business because I'm in... (Insert type of business here)" This of course is hogwash, but I do believe that if you are specifically doing business in the service industry, there are a few more things that you want to keep in mind. This will be a brief overview of some things that I think are very important, and you want to make sure you cover.

1) Clearly define your scope and schedule: There is an entire industry that has developed around Project Management. The one savior of every Project Manager in America is a phrase that I believe is branded on the forehead of every person who chooses that as their career field. "That is outside the scope of this project." Now when you work for the local computer company and are developing a computer lab for the ABC Corporation, you probably get to say that. However, I don't think that I have ever used that phrase in my 30 years of business. What I have said at certain instances is," You know I don't think we outlined that from the beginning, but if we can take a few minutes to work out the details I'll bet we can get that covered."

Someone who heard me say that recently responded with, "You mean it's outside the scope of the deal." Which, if I did not want to help the client or more importantly I didn't think that I could actually deliver, I could have used as my escape clause. Instead what I said was, "Absolutely not, but if we can take a few minutes and make sure that we have all of **our** expectations and reciprocations, than I can deliver for you more than what you need." The client stepped back and said. "Well sure we want to do that." For that phrase I was able to negotiate what essentially came out to about 45 minutes of additional labor and about $4,000 to my bottom line.

If I had known that this subject was going to be brought up I absolutely would have made sure that it was covered in advance, but since I hadn't ever heard of it, and they didn't think of it, we needed to make sure it got covered. The bottom line was that by going over as much as I can both in scope and schedule, we all would have been much happier. Now when it comes to scheduling there are two things that I would very strongly suggest you include in every planning session that you have. I call it the over/under.

It starts like this, if you are working for a client and everyone agrees that this job will take 5 weeks and you will be paid $125,000 for your work. The contracts are signed, everyone is happy and work begins. During the fourth week a decision point in the project is reached and you turn to the client and say, "We need to go right or left, here's what happens depending on what we do." The Client is in complete agreement that they understand and are comfortable with the information and therefore say," Let's go left." This is wonderful news for youe, because going right would have taken more time and effort than what was allocated.

Therefore when all is said and done you finish a week early. Everyone is happy, cigars are passed around, the champagne flows and the boss hands you a check for $100,000. Now what do you do? Your first instinct is probably to nudge the boss and politely ask for the other part of your payment. But the boss would then look at you and declare, well sure, but back when I turned left I shaved off a whole lot work on your part, and now you have another week to work with someone else." Sadly, he thinks he's actually doing you a favor.

Fortunately this falls back to your over/under in your contract, and since you are already familiar with that, it is covered in the contract that you negotiated. The Over/Under is what covers what happens to your pay if you produce the product in less time than you had planned. Some folks feel that since you finished early you should earn less, conversely some folks are afraid that if you finish early you will expect a bonus. Normally this isn't that big of an issue, but it has happened. Unfortunately what this usually will end up protecting you against is, what happens if a hurricane strikes, and your town is evacuated, so no one can do any work for a week, thus putting the whole project that far behind. How does that effect your pay or performances? If these things are covered in your initial contract than everyone should be satisfied with the results. However, no one, certainly not business owners, likes surprises. So take some extra time, make sure that you have everything covered that you can think of without having to have a legal interpreter explain your contract to your client.

2) Don't choose or be Chosen Based Strictly on Price:

I could give you an entire business course on pricing strategy and why you do and do not want to be the lowest priced guys on the block. But that's not why you're here, so let's see if I can give you the "abridged" version. Once upon a time there was some common business wisdom that went like this. "To live with the *Classes* you need to sell to the *masses*". Essentially telling you that if you could find the one product that everyone in America needed and find the best way to sell it to everyone in America, you would be wealthy beyond your wildest dreams. At the time, this was a valid statement. Then Sam Walton developed his business model which was successful to a point, unfortunately he died and his children warped it.

Personally, I like Sam Walton, I think he was brilliant and I encourage everyone to read his biography, but he's probably spinning end over end in his grave if he has any idea of what his kids have done with his store. One of the things you had to love about his business model was that he would get on TV and promise you that in any store X% of everything in it was made in America and you should check up on him. Today, it is my opinion, that if you can find anything in one of his stores that is made in America, it should he shown on TV.

Sam's kids decided that they had the power to buy in such large quantities that they could not only demand the lowest price for the item, but have, in fact, altered the way entire industries have do business, in the process. In doing so they created a whole new business model that puts entrepreneurs in a tight spot, one that you do not want to find yourself in. The pricing game is not a game that you or anyone else ever 'wins.' Unfortunately, even though they would argue otherwise, it is also a strategy where the customer will always become the loser. 'But I have to sell for lower than Joe's Garage down the street don't I?"

Not only do you not have to, but you don't even want to, let me explain why. First of all, remember even if you sat next to Joe in Auto Mechanics School you and he are not in competition anywhere but in your own minds. So stop thinking that way right now. Using the example of the garage, does your facility look like Joes? Do you have the same staff, the same waiting room, the same specialization or amenities as Joe? Although there may be some similarities in answers to the last question, amenities, is one of the most important.

The man who works on my car, I have been returning to for over 25 years. It started with a beat up old VW Rabbit; he specialized in VW at the time because he liked them, and he personally bought them, modified them and raced them for fun. Now by staying focused on the VW brand he was able to continue to provide outstanding service, and make an amazing discovery. When the college kids who came in with their beat up old VW's graduated and got jobs, they returned with BMW's and Mercedes. Therefore he was able to take his personal affection for a brand, and turn it into a draw for generations of drivers.

On the other side of the spectrum, you have your business developed and things are running rather well, but you are ready to take it up a notch. In order to do that you need that one big account, you want the fleet maintenance account for the vehicles that operate for "Big Company INC." So you draw up your proposal, developed around your strengths and specialties and have the appointment set for your initial presentation. The morning of your presentation one of your managers runs in and tells you that he had dinner with the sales guy from Joes Repair, who is currently servicing BCI's fleet and he said that he told your employee that their fleet price is 30% less than what you're about to pitch. What should you do with that information?

Well, the first thing that you don't do is go in to your presentation and cut all your prices by 40%. That's would be a very bad idea, for a number of reasons, but let's look at a few of the most outstanding:

a) If you do not have a huge mark up in your services than you can not afford to cut that much and stay in business.

b) Even if you can survive at this rate cut, if word got out, how would that effect the rest of your customers?

c) Do you want customers that are only coming to you because of price? The moment someone offers them a lower price, you have trained them to leave.

d) Most importantly, regardless of whether anyone else ever hears about this rate cut or not, you have just established your maximum price with this customer.

Our best bet is to wipe out the old adage about masses and classes, and instead try this on for new wisdom: *Do not involve yourself in a war you can not win, or in one that if won, you could not survive.* Translated that means, don't go head to head on a lower price, especially if you couldn't offer that lower price to the same customer without the competition of an alternate, lower price.

3) Tie your payment to clearly defined milestones:

Now you can probably tell that I am not a huge fan of this type of payment or work, but I understand that some industries established a series of standards and practices whereby 'contractor A' gets paid 10% now, 10% then and 80% when complete. I understand it; I just try not to get involved in it.

If you happen to find yourself in this type of business lets at least examine your options. The most common example that comes to MY mind is building contractors, if the house is $100,000, you get $30,00 to start, $20,000 when the walls are up, $30,000 when the roof is on and the remaining $20,000 upon completion. This is not a hard way to do business necessarily as long as these things are spelled out clearly. Unfortunately what hurts many of the folks working under these conditions are the elements and the calendar.

In addition to the roof, the walls and completion will be hitting those milestones on specific dates, or even times. Typically this only becomes a challenge when the contractor doesn't pad his estimate, the owner is on a tight schedule, or some natural disaster occurs. See the section on the over/under, but again this is something that you want to make sure is clearly spelled out so that there is not any question of who gets paid what, or when. Obviously one of the best ways to prevent these kinds of issues is to always make sure that you pad your time with 10% and your price with at least that much, unfortunately that isn't always possible. I can not tell you how often a customer who doesn't plan for an event properly, and the 'event' ends up either stalling or stopping a project while a solution is found. Unfortunately this will typically result in holding up the contractor the entire time. Not only forcing him to miss his date, but worse, possibly forcing him to ruin over budget so that he can maintain the crack quality staff that he has in place.

Plan for the best, but prepare for the worst and everyone will end up being happy.

4) Negotiate Ownership of the work up front: Most folks think that this refers specifically to creative folks and the work they produce, but it can refer to almost anyone. I was working for an event promoter once who had been putting on trade shows all over the south east. I got tied in because there was one specific trade show that I wanted to attend so I could make some good contacts.

He ran a raffle for his attendees, with the caveat that you must be present to win. The prizes had been donated by the exhibitors at the show and ranged from a $20 gift card to a large screen TV. One of the winners was not present for one of the mid level prizes so the promoter planned on 'donating the prize to charity.' Imagine his surprise and embarrassment when the vendor wanted his prize back. Now this may seem like a petty situation and one that should have been easily resolved, but how much easier would it have been if planned for in the beginning?

Moving back to the business involving the housing contractor, how could he prepare? It turns out that he employs one of the finest cabinet makers in the industry and when the owners come back and ask for a very specialized item, he sets 'his guy' to the task. In creating the solution he developed a cabinet combination that had never been seen before, essentially a cabinet that not only incorporated an interior "lazy Susan" for a rounded end cap, but also a specialized wine cooling system using all "green materials." The contractor thinks this is so neat he calls Architectural Digest Magazine who runs a cover story and suddenly the cabinet maker now has his own side business creating these specialized cabinets.

My question to you is, what percentage of his profits should go to the contactor, on whose time he designed and built these cabinets? What about the new owners who requested the designs and probably helped design them? Can you see just how quickly these things can spin out of control? I had a professor in college who's claim to fame was that he had over 97 patents in his name at a very large manufacturing concern here in the U.S. Just for curiosity several of us in class looked it up in the library. Now this professor lived in a nice little house for he and his wife in a quiet little town and drove a 20 year old car.

After finding out all the 'commonly used items' he was involved in developing we were amazed, why wasn't he living the 'high life' somewhere? Very simply, his employment contract with the manufacturing company required him to sign over the rights to all his inventions created on their time clock. This gentleman who probably should have been a multi billionaire, earned a little less than $60,000 a year teaching at the community college.

Negotiate everything up front, leave nothing to chance, as much as I love and respect my father's way of doing business, a handshake will not help you in court.

Obviously these ideas may not apply across the board to all businesses, perhaps not even all service providers, but these are points that I have seen occur in the past. Some of these things happen to the betterment of a project but to the detriment of the providers. You work very hard for what you do, your ideas are valuable, you need to make sure that you get paid for the work you do. Almost as important you want to make sure that you retain the rights to that work for future ventures.

You may have done a great deal of work for JV partner X this year, and once he is done, he will probably move on to the next JV partner and if she doesn't bring your project back to life, that doesn't mean that an idea is dead. A week a month or 5 years from now, you may find one or two small changes that you could make to a project and start it all over and this time, the project is yours, and because you retained the rights to your intellectual property, the profits are now all yours.

Even if you don't see yourself as a "service provider" or in a service industry, I would be surprised if you carefully looked over these ideas, that you couldn't find that most of these ideas will work in your business as well. Remember the one phrase that you should never use in relation to your business is: "But that wont work here, I'm in the XYZ business." Remember the business is to turn a profit and keep your customers coming back. In that way, all businesses are on equal footing.

Jerome L. Hess

14. Big dreams mean Big Challenges

Nothing big was ever accomplished by small thinkers. In the same vein, gamble big, lose big. This is not meant as a warning, because as you read this you're going to stop at least once and say, "Yeah but I thought you said...". You're right; I probably did say something contradictory, because in the end the only 100 percent valid statement that will run through this entire section is to do something. Big or small, do something.

I started in the 5th grade with a lemonade stand made from wood I 'borrowed' from a building site, using resources provided by my mom. That's just about as shoe string as you can get with out standing beside an exit ramp with a sign and a cup. Yet even then I had grand ideas, you see the lemonade stand idea came from 'Dennis the Menace.' My next inspiration was from a little farther up the ladder.

I was a Cub Scout and we were encouraged to sell "Grit", now to this day I really haven't a clue what "Grit" is other than that stuff in your teeth when you've been mowing the lawn for too long, so it wasn't really something I wanted to do. However on the back page of that sample copy of "Grit" that my Den Mother had was an advertisement that could have changed my life forever.

This was the early Seventies and my mom was a stay at home wife of a Naval Officer who had the time to do things like, mail out Christmas cards, and clean house. There on the back of

Grit was an entire page of prizes that one could earn by selling; you guessed it, Christmas Cards. Now understand I was the kid who saw the ad on the back on the comic book for the submarine for $19.99 and got *really* excited about it. So the details didn't mean nearly as much as the Radio Controlled Plane or the 'Real' Bow and Arrow kit or even (cue the music) the **Telescope.** I had always wanted a Telescope, I had just started my lifetime love of science fiction, the Apollo landings had been successful and I was ready for liftoff.

After begging for over an hour my Den Mother was kind enough to tear off the back page and let me take it home with me. Although to this day I don't know what upset her more, the fact that I wanted to tear her "sample" or the fact that I was not interested in being a glorified paper boy. My cousin in Chicago was a paperboy and in the winter his dad had to help him deliver papers, regardless of the fact that I lived in Florida, it looked like to much work. But this, this seemed to be a slam dunk way toward the beginnings of the Astronaut corp.

To make a long story short, Dad co-signed the agreement with me, and did his duty as a dad and ordered 3 boxes of cards, I'm sure mom still has them somewhere. After everything was mailed off dad taught me about "the fine print." You see the ad listed all the great prizes and even talked about how inexpensive the cards could be, you got to choose whether you earned cash or prizes, but it didn't say how many boxes of cards you would need to sell to earn each prize. If memory serves me, one telescope equaled 97 boxes of Christmas cards. My father then explained that with a neighborhood of over 200 homes I only needed to sell to every other family in order to get my telescope.

Wait, I had to go knock on doors? Well I had been doing it for my Catholic School twice a year for 5 years so far, so how much different could this be? Truth be told for the first 10 or 12 houses it was a snap, then one mom said, "Roy didn't tell me the school was selling Christmas cards?" Then it all came home, they thought I was selling for the school, and being an honest 10 year old I couldn't allow that to continue, so sales got somewhat tougher after that house.

When all was said and done, and my Aunts and Uncles had been called and I spent a Saturday morning in Dad's Real Estate office (he started in Real Estate 2 years before he retired from the Navy), I found that I had sold 127 boxes of Christmas cards, more than enough to launch my career! You have never seen a boy more excited. Then came the rest of the small print. This being the middle of the 1970's, no one used Credit Cards, and therefore my prize would not arrive until 90 – 120 days after all my Christmas Cards had been delivered. Worse yet, delivery would be an additional 8 to 12 weeks to allow for printing, shipping and handling. I couldn't see Mars until the 6th Grade, and by then who knew if NASA would even still be accepting applications!

What in the world does all this have to do with your starting or re-starting your career as an Entrepreneur? Everything, as my dad always said, "There is a lesson to be learned in everything that you do." You may have never sold magazines, or donuts or Christmas cards or even had a lemonade stand, but the chances are good that somewhere along in your growing years you were face to face with something that turned into you performing some good or service and someone giving you money in return. Whether it was selling candy bars for the Mighty Mite football league, or Car Washes for the Boosters, you were involved. What you may not have known is just how much you were involved or how big the venture you were actually involved in was to the folks who ran it.

The company who I sold Christmas cards for in 1977 is the same company that you or your spouse probably visits each year to buy your Barbie and Start Trek ornaments from in the mall. Yes that company, started as one of the largest fund raising entities in America. What most people don't know is that they didn't start as a card company; they were a 'mid level' printing company who came up with the idea of utilizing the kids of middle class America as their greatest sales force.

All I wanted then was a telescope, but the folks at the printing company were looking at the bigger picture, they were envisioning the day when you and I would call them personally and custom order our Christmas Cards. Now I don't know how many folks actually order or mail Christmas cards, but I can tell you that this particular company has been able to turn the Internet into their personal "print on demand" service. Allowing folks from all over the world to custom design and print their own Holiday cards, celebrating holidays on almost every day of the year. Today for example is "Take your Pants for a Walk Day." According to one source; *"Give your pants some exercise. After all, they are looking a little tight around the middle. The walk will do them good."*

But how does that apply to you exactly? We all start somewhere, and we all have more than one way we can start. I have one advisor who extols the virtue of "Good Enough." Claiming that far too many creative folks will toil and work over a single project (like a book) until every comma and indent is in its grammatically perfect position. He on the other hands claims that as long as it doesn't look like your 5 year old wrote it, send it out! I'm not saying I agree wholeheartedly, but I have a feeling that by this point you may have spotted at least one or two typos.

So, you are ready to start your business, you have your idea somewhat fleshed out, your partner is on board with it, now what should you do? As you may have guessed I am a big believer in the idea that you should "start small and reinvest your profits" idea of business development. I will admit that this is not appropriate for every single type of business nor is it right for every single person. After all what would the NYC skyline look like today if Donald Trump worked that way? Let's just say it would be significantly shorter. However, unless your plan is to build a 97 story building, lets see what you can do about starting your investment with only as much money as you can absolutely afford to lose.

I don't want you to think that I have no confidence in you, but I also don't want to think that you have to rent an office, hire a staff and outfit everyone with the latest computing devices before you can ever open your doors! One of my favorite serial Entrepreneurs is a young lady we'll call Liz, Liz is a single mom who really only wanted the best for her child but knew that she couldn't depend on "a man" to provide for her. While at the same time, some careers, like Real Estate, were just not her cup of tea.

I call Liz a "serial Entrepreneur" because since her daughter was born she has been an Artist, a wood worker, a collector and re-seller of collectables, a Vintage Clothing shop owner and now is a unique upper middle class restaurateur. By that I mean that the food she delivers is simple, but of such a high quality and delivered in such an amazing atmosphere, that she is able to charge more than the fast food joint down the street. Since one does not typically just abandon one's 'vintage clothing' collection when one changes directions, Liz has actually devoted a part of her restaurant to the display area for her vintage items, as well as a space that local artists can come and perform.

Now if you had told Liz 10 years ago that she would own a restaurant one day she would have told you that you were crazy, but I strongly believe that it was stepping up, slowly but surely from business to business, until she one day had the opportunity to open a restaurant, it almost seems as though it was part of a master plan. When she told me what her idea was, the only thing that I could even think to suggest was that she harness some of her copy writing ability, and make her marketing look like something no one else had ever seen as well as generate a 'character' to represent her restaurant, so she could use a common theme in her marketing. Not only has she created a character to use in her marketing she has posters, t-shirts and beach towels (she's in a resort town) with her character and his "sayings".

So, in one location she has a dine in or take out restaurant, a vintage clothing line (also available on the internet), a line of personalized 'adware' (also available on the net) and a character that can be used at almost any event around town, all of which can generate income. Looking at the quality of what she has established almost anyone would step back and be in awe at her fund raising abilities, after all these things cost a fortune right?

Not always, even in resort towns, even on the boardwalk, there are always one or two store fronts that are either so special use or so oddly shaped, that they never can stay rented. So why not approach the owner and suggest that you fill it, either on a contingency basis or in a profit sharing plan with the owner, or ad generation trade, or even a time spent proration. In this case the rent was waived for the first 90 days, and then the ensuing rent would be based on 125% of the county average, for that same size space. Notice she didn't negotiate on what kind of use, but on square footage, the most level playing field available. Also of note is that although her rent would end up 'above average', it was delayed 90 days, enough time to determine the validity of her idea.

Although restaurant equipment isn't exactly falling from the sky, if you approach most vendors and offer to position them in your ads for temporary use of their older or outdated equipment, it can be had for almost no money down. As creative as she is, Liz performed all the physical 'rehabbing' herself, for which it could not have turned out better, leaving only her raw materials as her initial outlay. Can you think of another way to open a restaurant on the boardwalk of a resort for under $1000 investment? Right, neither could I, but she did it, and today on her 3rd anniversary she will tell you it's the best thing she could have done. Her daughter having just past her 16th year can now work behind the counter as a regular, although part time, employee. Before that who do you imagine was filling out the costume when the character was needed?

Having worked in real estate I can tell you that I have seen more than my fair share of restaurants fail, so what did Liz have at stake, beyond her pride? The initial $1000 raw material investment, several weeks of hard and creative labor, and that is all. If a hurricane had blown through on her 3rd day of business and shut her down she would be out her initial raw materials investment, but even that, only if she hadn't opened on one of the biggest holiday weekends of that resort area. By the 2nd day she was scrambling for more raw materials (food etc), because she had sold almost completely out of her pantry in the first two days. It's not every day that a restaurant can be so 'well thought out' as to "sell out" within 48 hours, but when you plan for success everything can go your way.

So what is it that you have in mind? How big is your idea? The title of the chapter indicates that big dreams can be hard, and if that's what you read it to mean, you're right. They *can* be hard, it *can* be dangerous, you *can* lose everything, but it doesn't have to be like that, with a little advance preparation you can make your worst nightmare little more than a faint memory. One of the best ways is to decide in advance what the absolute maximum amount you can lose, that would not ruin your life. Now there are some folks that feel that this is the same way that some people see a prenuptial agreement, an expectation of failure.

But it's not, instead its setting your budget, a budget that is set for the worst, but prepared for the best. Yet even when considering the worst, you must plan for the best scenario you can, how much can you afford to lose and not expect your wife to leave you and your home to be foreclosed upon. Please do not think that this is any way to discourage you from dreaming big and betting big, however I would also ask you to plan and be, smart. When Walt Disney decided that he was going to open a theme park, right next to his ultra successful Disney World, but one that instead was aimed at parents and have few if any 'rides', he had to lay out a huge budget for his project. Walt had more than enough challenges in 'selling' this idea to his board of directors, can you imagine if he had walked in without any solid data to help him demonstrate both the negative and the positive? Folks are used to being 'sold' the blue sky', if you demonstrate the 'hard ground' as well, you show your prepared.

So, you are a better than average Real Estate Salesman, you have got some inside information on a 21 unit building that is going to come up for sale and if 'worked' properly could be bought for 10 cents on the dollar. But even at 10 cents your investment is going to be over 1.2 Million dollars. Most folks could sell everything they and their spouses own and could not come up with a fraction of that much money. What would you do? Would you walk away and hope another deal comes along? Would you borrow against the building itself, maybe not getting the 10% deal, but even if you were at 30 cents on the dollar, could you show how the math could work? Would you look for partners? Do you have a plan for that?

Here are a few ideas for what you might consider:
1) You walk away, and understand that another deal will come by someday.
2) You could seek out some partners.
3) You could secure an "option" and try and flip the building.
4) You could hit up every bank on the eastern seaboard and look for at least one of them with cash to lend.

Option number 1 is not uncommon, and although it isn't the best idea, it is indeed the safest. After all a project like this is really thinking big for your very first 'deal' in your own real estate company. Maybe you should start looking for smaller properties to start with, and slowly build up the capital needed. That way when you do find your next 'big' deal, you will have the 'money in the bank, and the reputation in place.

Partners are not a bad idea; they are one way to spread around the risk. Unfortunately at the very least, they are a way to dilute your profits and at the worst they are another avenue through which you may lose everything. Or you might see it squandered away through mismanagement, or in a worse case scenario it becomes the center of a legal issue for which there seems to be no end. Partners are not negative in all cases, however, in my experience the one thing that makes a partnership work well, is a rock solid contract.

Securing an option on a building like this is actually a pretty good opportunity. One of my largest mortgage deals occurred in a very similar fashion. Now I will admit that there are a great number of things that all came into alignment to make this happen, but in the mid 80's my company was able to buy an option on a condo, and sell the building before the option expired. We were also able to handle the financing for the new owners (it was part of the enticement to buy), and walked away with huge profits. Believe it or not, as well balanced as everything was, the entire project balanced on the value of a portable computer.

In the last example you could spend quite a bit of your own time and money seeking your own financing, so that you could walk away with your own project, in your own name. Unfortunately what you will undoubtedly find is that by the end of week two of your search, many of the banks already know who you are and why your calling. A "good deal" is one of the fastest moving pieces of information that gets distributed on the planet.

Unless your first bank is the one that gives you the money, the bankers will begin to talk amongst themselves, and the chances are good that if one bank in an area is unable to finance it, most of the rest of them will be unable to as well.

But it is your business, so lets take one step back and take a look at the bigger picture. What is it that you are trying to accomplish? Do you want to do one big deal, or do you want to open your own Real Estate Investment business that will provide for you and your family for the next several generations? If you're looking for a long term business then let me say that I have not seen another series of events come together like the condo I flipped, in the 25 years since. So your in this for the long haul, the size of your initial investment, this is what you risk, and that risk is dependent somewhat on where you are and what your specific talents are.

Using myself as an example, you're in your late 30's, somewhat over weight, and on your 3rd career since college. Now that's not your 3rd job, but your 3rd career. Since you graduated college you have relearned or re-purposed your skill set on at least 3 separate occasions, possibly more. Currently you feel that your skills are being used in the right industry, but you see a specific niche in that industry that you feel is being under serviced. In your case it just so happens to be middle age dual income couples with a few kids, but who have lost their home in the recent Real Estate "adjustment' that the country experienced. Therefore their credit is perhaps less than stellar. Your thought being that if you could buy a building like what you found, you could spend the rest of your life selling those units to your niche and retire comfortably. But that's not really your style is it, your too young to retire, and even if the money were available you would want to 'stay in the game.'

So, lets see how we can get started on a perpetual business that will continue to feed you long after the first 21 units have been sold. Like many folks you and your wife each have a retirement fund and you own you cars, but not your home, and due to loan to value ratios borrowing against the house are just not an option. Ask yourself, what you need to get started? Do you *need* and office? Do you *need* to own your own office equipment? Do you *need* staff? Other than the staff part I will be the first to say that they are nice to have, but when you're getting started not required. As far as the staff goes, I cant even say that, that would be nice to have. So how can you get started?

You're a Real Estate investor, a great deal of your business will be done in one of three places: The Property your buying, the Title Company and the Loan Company. If you find yourself in **need** of an office you typically will find that for a small fee, and if they have the room, your Title Company will rent/loan you and office, but even if they can't I receive about 10 offers a week from different companies around the city that own buildings 2with no one renting them, therefore they can often rent them to you on a low fee for a daily or weekly rate. Typically you would almost prefer hourly, but that's a whole different business.

You need a way to be reached and a way to reach folks, so you do need a phone of some kind. Today the options for a telephone and service are almost mind numbing. I have seen valid 6 figure business's run from everything from a "Majik Jack" to a full blown "Wizard Phone system" from the boys in blue. We have found that in many cases when you are just starting a business your communications needs will be pretty simple, and can often be met with a "pay as you go" cell phone and a 3rd party 800 line that can receive faxes. The cell phone will not have all the gizmo's and games, but it can also cost as little as $20 a month for full service telephone service.

You will probably want to invest in some kind of technology, more and more business is being done online, and whether you personally agree with it or not, it is out there. When I started my mortgage business the IBM PC was still just a good idea, nothing was standard and everything was expensive. Today the $200 netbook that I just got an ad for will do everything that a $500 desktop will do; Kodak has a Multi function, color, wifi printer/ fax/ scanner for under $150. There is more than enough open source software (open Office.org) as well as online alternatives (Google docs), that can meet almost 100% of your software needs for almost zero cost.

There is a particular print company that we all get emails and postcards from that will print and deliver color business cards for under $20. Letterhead and stationary is very nice looking but completely UN needed. As a point of information that same country an print your logo on hats, t-shirts and golf shirts for very reasonable costs, in case you want to wear some media.

Many of your netbooks now include a built in "web cam" don't depend on it invest an additional $20 on a nice digital camera, and perhaps even another $100 for a 'flip cam' video camera. Perhaps not a requirement, but it could be a nice option.

We are now down to your two largest investments, and you may already own them, however updating or replacing can occasionally pay off as well. First off, one of your largest and most important investments (for this particular type of business) would be a good reliable car. We could also say it need to be fuel efficient and have AC and a half dozen other specs, but really as long as it looks good, runs and can keep you looking presentable, it will work. There was a time when most folks would tell you that you needed to lease the most prestigious Cadillac on the fleet have leather seats and...none of that is needed. Wanted, desired, maybe even feel nicer, but certainly would not allow you to earn even one nickel more. I knew one investor in the late 90's who's goal was to never have a client ever ride in his car.

Finally, and again, you may have this, but even if you do you may want to upgrade it, a good suit, 2 pairs of slacks 3 different shirts 4 ties and a nice clean pair of hard shoes. With that kind of setup, you can almost do laundry Monday's and Thursdays and never have to look back. There have been many differing opinions on how you should dress for business, but as far as I'm concerned as long as "Dress for Success" is still being printed, you still want to wear a suit for business. You can always dress down by taking off your coat and rolling up your sleeves, but if you're in a khaki and polo shirt there's not much you can do to bring that look into the board room.

I think that we now have our real estate investment business open and operational and we have done it for an initial investment well under $1000 (barring a new car). Now my question to you is this: Can you start working on your business, in this case Real Estate investment, in your spare time, without quitting your day job, and expect to yield positive results? There are many "businesses" where you can't but our Real Estate Investor has only to look up and he is in business. I personally have seen investors generate an ongoing income of 6 figures while still working 40 hours a week for someone else. Therefore as long as that initial $1000 didn't come from left handed Louie's loan service, you should have a pretty safe investment.

Finally I would ask that you take note of the one word that I have continued to use throughout this book when referring to the money it takes, and that word is Investment. The moment you begin to understand that you are not "dumping your money into" something, but are instead Investing in your business and your future, everything about your business will begin to change. You will find that you look at your expenditures much differently. Instead of 'having to spend $300" on a laptop you are investing $300 on a vital piece of equipment that you need to make your business successful.

Conversely, if someone comes to you and wants you to 'expand your business' into a line of products that you're not familiar with, you will be able to take a step back and say, "I have a budget of $1,000, should I invest it in this new product line, or re-invest it in my business to help increase profits?" Now there will definitely be times that you will want to expand your business to include other, new ideas. But remember if your budget was $1000 and this new idea is going to need an investment of ½ your budget, you have just decreased your survivability by a certain percentage.

Let's go back to the restaurant, Liz already has expanded into several ventures other than food, but they were all areas that she was familiar with, that she had the inventory to fulfill and that was not going to subtract anything from her operating budget. But if her neighbor in the boardwalk had suggested that she have an open mike night or a 'poetry slam' in order to bring in more foot traffic, I would have several questions for the neighbor. The first being, if it's such a great idea why font you do it? My next question would be, does this neighbor have or now where to 'borrow' the PA system needed to assure that the vocals can be heard? If not understand its eating at your budget. Finally, what kind of increase would an event like this put on her marketing expenses? Yes, she could put a sign in the window, but is that really going to be enough to make a difference in foot traffic? Probably not.

But let's say that Liz thinks that this is a great idea, however being a smart business owner she knows that her budget didn't really include anything like this, how could she make it happen? Well PA systems are easy, although you could buy one second hand at a Pawn Shop, the chances are good that if her neighbor doesn't have one, she can rent a set for less than $30 for the evening. Next would be her marketing efforts. Liz has already printed up her materials for the next 3 months, what can she do? Well, although the sign in her window may not make a HUGE difference, one in her window and her neighbors windows, would double the exposure. Additionally she could some and hour one afternoon talking to the rest of the store owner on the boardwalk. Also, the community has a newspaper a library, a music store and an FM pop station.

The newspaper would be simple; an hour's creative effort to write a good press release could garner her one or 2 column inches in the weekend section. By harnessing the "character" that she created, and asking if he could be interviewed would provide GREAT exposure for the event. Additionally, since its open microphone and poetry slam the local library would probably allow her to place small flyers out. Also instead of having a comedy open mike night if she opened it up to singer/songwriters she could undoubtedly get an interview on the morning show and perhaps even the afternoon drive. Finally, all of these items can be documented and added to the businesses website for viewing. Now she has just generated far more that $1000 in advertising for her business and helped the rest of the shop owners bring in more foot traffic as well!

So, we have just developed a pretty good idea, we hope, into an event, with a great deal of media coverage, all for little or no money. For the first night we have $30 in PA rental and let's say $10 in copying fees, so that everyone can get a flyer. However, as we have discussed, even the best laid plans of mice and entrepreneurs, is open to interpretation. If your mice can't read, then you may be in big trouble.

What if, after your first quarter you discover that the $1000 is gone, and your income, even with the open mike night just hasn't been growing? What do you do know? There are a number of answers, and as a book on entrepreneurs you would think that it's my job to tell you to "push on". But its not, my job here is to try and help you create a business of your own, without killing yourself, draining all your resources or causing your family to leave you. You and your partner looked at everything before you got started, you were able to come up with the $1000 without having to borrow, hopefully you started without quitting your day job, but your first quarter, even with a holiday weekend, was dismal. Yes I would say, "Try whatever you can to make it another quarter", 3 months is not really enough time for folks to find and return to or make a habit of a new restaurant. But it is your business and your investment.

When you started you were able to generate the $1000, you now have about $100 left, what should you do? First call an executive meeting between you and your partner. Now I'm not talking about a business partner (hopefully you don't have one of those) I'm talking about your life partner. If you are single, who did you talk to about your business in the 1st place? Who was your mentor? That's the partner you want to talk this over with. If your wife was not involved in the initial planning she needs to be now. Because now the big decisions are about to be made. You spent your initial investment, you're not breaking even, assuming you have been keeping a good set of books, can you even see an upward trend?

That holiday weekend should have been huge, but aside from that, how has the rest of the weekends gone? Are folks coming in, are they coming back? You tried the open mike night so at least you are full on Sunday's, are these folks making purchases? Are you selling more food or more Vintage items? Where is the income, whatever income you have generated, come from? You may have a restaurant and after 90 days find out that you have a GREAT place for vintage clothing and maybe a coffee bar or internet café? Maybe your focus is on the wrong thing? Maybe your location is bad? Are the neighbors making any money, are there any restaurants in the area that are in the black?

As much as you want to stick it out and keep plodding on, if, after your $1000 is gone, and you and your partner talk, what do they see as happening? For example, you may feel that things are bound to pick up, but if you're spending 50 hours at your job plus another 30 hours at the store, when are you having time for your family? More importantly. Looking at your books, how long will it be before, mathematically, you can see yourself actually leaving your day job? Sure the restaurant may be able to survive the first year and perhaps even turn a profit, but if i9t has to pay you $40,000 so you can devote your full attention to it and have a home life, how long, according to your books, will that be? I have a friend who is a cabinet maker, he worked for a company all day and spent 6 hours every night making cabinets on his own to sell at a profit, which he did. But he was such a skilled worker that in order for him to leave his day job he had to be able to pay himself, $45,000 a year, just to replace his day income. Now he was actually earning more than the 45 during the day, but after all things considered he and his wife decided that at $45 he could leave. Unfortunately the math said that at his current rate of manufacture, he would work for 17 years before that happened. Unfortunately that's not exactly what he wanted, nor was his wife willing to wait that long to see him again.

So what does your business have in store for you? Remember the idea is to own a business that gives you freedom to grow and learn and be in control of your destiny, not to become yet another employee to a job you just happen to own. Just as important, if the initial investment actually represented a hardship or a major portion of what you had available, how long can you afford to re invest that money? You and I both know that to open a restaurant on a budget like that is very difficult, but as we have shown, and seen, it is not impossible. However you do need a few things to happen to make it work. You need to become profitable in a relatively short period of time. You need to have items with a higher than average margin of profit. Most of all, you need to be able to invest the time, money and efforts into creating enough of a commotion as to continually drive in customers.

Here in Florida there was a business venture once where a certain company would buy hot dog carts by the dozen, stock them, get them licensed and then put very attractive young ladies in very small swimsuits beside major highways selling hot dogs. I personally didn't understand how this could be possible or profitable, until I was told that the hot dogs cost the customer $5 each and the girls worked 100% from tips. Here you had a high margin item, the hot dogs may have cost 50 cents to fully assemble and sell, and low overhead, after the purchase and license of the cart everything else worked off of what was sold. In practice it was almost a no lose investment for the business owners. Until some folks got to the county board and decided that these young ladies were a distraction and I was actually dangerous to have them along major thoroughfares. You can fight city hall, but its VERY expensive to win. In the end the company sold the hot dog carts, at a profit, to end owners, because they were licensed ad had a spot already, many traditional business owners invested in them. When they found out that the young ladies in swim suits could no longer sell them, most were turned into more traditional carts with more traditional hot dogs, but people bought them all out. The initial company made a great deal of profit for a year, and then made even more profit when they no longer saw it as a profitable venture. Somewhat win/win.

The bottom line is this. You are investing in a business. The goal is to have a great business, quit your day job and make lots of money. The reality is, that occasionally you can do everything right, and profits still aren't what you need them to be, you must have an exit strategy, that will allow you to exit with your dignity and your life savings intact. Typically when you hear someone's sob story about how they bought a widget manufacturing business and invested their life savings and are now broke, you are looking at some folks who did not perform their due diligence on the front end.

But you are different, you did your homework, you and your partner know what your bottom line is, and you know when the time is to leave gracefully. Please don't take that with too much humor, if the need comes to leave you do not want to upset anyone on your way out, these things have a way of haunting you later in life. So you have examined the books, looked at the future and the math just does not seem as though it will work in your favor. One thing to keep in mind, this is a business, not your child. I will move heaven and earth to help make my son a success, my business, well I can always start another one, and so can you. Fall in love with the process not the product. Unless this is your great grandmother 12 generations back famous cookie recipe, no one will really get hurt if your business expires, and that's the way it should be. There comes a point where mathematically you need to be prepared to move on. Remember if this was a good idea there is a **great** idea out there waiting for you. But you can have the greatest ideas in the world, but if you leave a trail of decimation and destruction in the wake of your first business you may never be able to open a second business.

Most of America's successful business men have been Serial Entrepreneurs. They started with one thing, and through a process of pass and fail, ended up as the giant we all remember them as becoming. Ray Kroc, AL Williams, Colonel Sanders, Donald Trump, they all started in one place, and through a series of trials and tribulations ended up on top in some place completely different. Keep your reputation, your dignity and most of all your integrity intact and there will be a second chance available to you. I once knew a man who upset so many people on his way out of one business that he opened the next one in his wife's name. That seemed to go well, for a while, then it to became a casualty. It was almost amusing when he did it again in 3 of his children's names, on 3 different occasions. I say almost because the way it was discovered was when the youngest son got married and tried to buy a car. Lets just say that's one Thanksgiving dinner I would have avoided.

The bottom line is to determine what your maximum investment can be, and then do everything you can to stick to it. I'm not saying that it's easy, watching your business go down is almost like watching a child lose a race, so first try not to get emotionally involved to that level. Yes you do need to be willing to commit to making your business a success, and yes one of the biggest regrets many businessmen have is looking back saying "If only I...", so if you have to make the decision to keep on or cut and run, make sure you have done your due diligence. Meet with your partner and go over everything you have done, and everything you could do, and see if there is anything that you may have missed. Often times if your life partner is not associated with the day to day operation of the business you can get a completely fresh perspective. If you have that ability, do NOT dismiss any idea they may suggest. Remember you have been so focused on this thing that maybe you have developed a set of blinders, if you have the chance to get a fresh look at the business take it.

I know many folks who, in the planning stages of their business determine what their absolute maximum investment can be over the next six months, and then set their initial operating budget at ½ that amount. Yes you're probably going to be running tight; yes you're not going to be able to do everything that you want to do for advertising and promotions that will force you to get creative. I knew a restaurateur who owned a place right on the beach, but at night and when the weather was bad, he had no business. For almost 90 complete days every year there were no customers in his store. Many of his fellow restaurateurs decided that this was a great time to take a vacation, some weekends his was the only place to get food for over a mile, yet he still had empty tables.

In talking it over with his partner, who was not part of the business, he discovered, as many have, that the greeting card companies have a day of celebration every single day of the year (today for example is National Lasagna Appreciation day, what a great idea for a restaurant) and so in researching the off beat holidays he decided that he would create, low cost marketing events surrounding these holidays. For example, on Robert Goddard's Birthday (the inventor of the modern rocket) he had a model rocket launching contest. His restaurant was the site where over 20 rockets went up that day; you could see the plumes of smoke from over a mile away. But better yet, he gave each contestant a hand full of 50% off coupons to put in each rocket. As the rockets reached their maximum height, some as high as a quarter mile UP, the parachutes deployed and out came the coupons. To flutter and fall to the ground, some were found as far as 3 miles away. He had 20 families eating because of the contest, and when it was all over, stated that he had had another 17 coupons redeemed over the next 10 days.

In the end he was finally able to start to turn his business around, now he has a steady flow of locals who come to his restaurant rain or shine, and he has the bonus influx of the tourists. But what if he hadn't been able to turn it around? Restaurants are not inexpensive to get started for most folks, what if you determine after 6 months, or a year or 5 years, that you have reached your maximum investment, how do you make the decision to stop or continue on? The best way, and the least emotional is to determine it mathematically. If you were wise enough in the beginning to establish you maximum possible investment for the first year, and stuck to it, the math makes everything much easier.

For example, you owned the restaurant on the beach, the monthly lease on your equipment is $5,000, your rent is $2,000, your recurring expenses (power, staff etc) are another $2,000 per month, you now know that on the first day of every month you must earn $9,000, before you can break even, remember most business owners do not pay themselves first, they try and survive on what's left over, so you're not drawing a paycheck at $9,000. If your total maximum investment was $100,000 and you determined to hold back half for emergencies, then at the 12 month point you are probably looking at expenses of $108,000. Without considering your income. If you have been close to 'breaking even' and had an income averaging $63,000 for the year, you have gone through $22,000 of your initial $50,000. This is the $13,000 difference plus an assumption of an initial $9,000 outlay.

As it stands now, if nothing changes, you should be able to make it through another year or so, but then what? Then it comes to math, remember initially you set aside $100,000 that you could afford to invest, some folks would say "lose", without affecting your ability to retire at some point in life. How do you start your second year? Do you start your second year? Remember we have talked about some options; you could sell a portion of the business that might be tough at this point. You may be able to bring in external partners, not a favorite of mine. Or you could look for the "little" things to change? However, the one thing that most folks don't address is something that were going to talk about next, and that is, changing your marketing.

Right now, your back is not up against the wall, but you do want to start looking at how you can change things, a little bit at a time, and continue to operate. Since you have at least one more years worth of 'buffer' most instincts are to use it. Bailing out now would do little other than tarnishing your business reputations, thus making it very difficult to ever get another business started in that community again. So, tighten your belt, cut back on your benefits and lets see how we can bring more customers into the restaurant.

For some folks closing a business would mean that they have 'failed', those are the people who "fell in love" with their business. The only problem with that is the effect that it can have on you and the rest of your life as changes occur. Both negative and positive changes can make a difference to your whole world, if you are that emotionally invested in your business. Become passionate about what you do, but be sure to keep enough distance from the project emotionally so that if, the day should ever come where you need to push the 'off' button you can do so without injuring yourself or anyone around you.

Afterword

Here you have it over 200 pages with a collection of some of the most eclectic tools you never knew you needed to start your own business. I have been involved with the launch of several companies, some very large, some, just me and the wall, if I had a book, like this one that had everything collected in one place, I could have saved myself many frightened days and more than a few sleepless nights. Instead I learned a great deal of this as I went through it

The number one thing that I learned was that the best and most comprehensive source of knowledge bar none is to find a mentor, someone who I was responsible to, to learn from and recount to, from that point onwards, I have never had a business in place where I had less than one mentor, but I have experienced greater success and less stress in business and almost no bleed over into my home life at all.

A mentor allows you to test new ideas, and find out new tools that may be available to one person but not the other. Additionally the opportunity to have someone that you can be completely honest and accountable to is worth more than you will ever understand, until you find yourself in a situation where you need someone of that caliber. Your "best bud" is probably not your best choice there, you need someone who will tell you "That is a really bad idea," when its needed. But you also need someone that will be able to help keep you on the right path, when all else seems to be failing.

221

Jerome L. Hess

If you will grab on to the ideas that have been presented to you here, study them, and be willing to perform your due diligence than there is no reason why your business should not move as smoothly and self assuredly as is possible.

I wish I could guarantee you success, but there isn't anyone who can do that. What I can tell you is that if you will create a plan for yourself and your business, research your ideas and put your tools in their proper place, you can give yourself an advantage. This advantage is precisely what you need to bring your business through the test of time, money, and adversity that will be presented before you every day. With this kind of preparation you will surely be able to then follow it through to the doorway of success.

Many people stand on the edge of success seeming to wait for someone to 'give them permission' to enter. If that's you than I not only give you permission, I tell you that it is your responsibility to go forward and create business of such magnitude that it completely fulfills everything that you need in life. I also grant you the permission to develop your business to the point where it will take you into whatever realm of success you wish to attain. You don't need anyone's permission, but if you're waiting for it, you now have it.

222

MY RESOURCES

We now come to that place in the book where some folks start to wonder how we got all this information? Could one person have ever really done all of these things? The answer is not only yes, but I have actually pulled them from my own work experience. Oh you've heard about the restaurant owner and the dog polisher, and just about everything in between, but let me state emphatically that as your days seem shorter than longer, you will find yourself with more hours to rest than hours to work.

So what can you do? Believe it or not my first recommendation is to look for a new coaching staff. A new group of folks who you can confer with and to whom you will not only be completely honest with but to whom you will be completely accountable. You will find that complete accountability will allow you to reveal and be revealed some of the things that although you consider 'small' may actually be the lynchpins of your changes. One of the first things you will want to work on with this group are the things that you really can change. In this particular case my recommendation is to go find a Mentor. Even if things are going great, if you don't have a mentor, go find one.

My first mentor helped me accomplish almost everything in my life that I have accomplished. My dad, Charles J. Hess, Jr. spent over 20 years serving his country in the US Navy. He chose to retire after 23 years because the "part time" job he was working was out earning his salary by a factor of 2 or

3 times. However, even with all that success he still made sure that I was in a position to learn any and everywhere possible. One of his biggest lessons revolved around the idea that as good as money could be, the one thing that truly mattered in this world was family.

Next would be Phil Strack. We met Phil almost 20 years ago, I was building one business, he was in a comparable business and I needed some help. A mutual friend introduced us, as much as I hate to admit it, Phil and my dad had a great deal in common when it came to business. Phil built one company from a staff of 1 all the way to several teams that covered several counties. A few years later he realized that what he really wanted was to find a way to manage his kid's sports teams, and not have to miss another game. Over the years he was able to transition from one business into another with out any one losing out. Additionally he has served as an excellent example of how a working man should treat his family.

Finally, Joe Pici, one of the finest example of a rock solid businessman who is willing to extend a hand and help you up, regardless of whether you feel you deserve it or not. Joe has taught all over the world, as a corporate and business trainer, yet he has never allowed all that notoriety and acclaim to "go to his head." Joe is an excellent example of a business man, family man and mentor.

There are dozens and dozens of folks throughout the years who have never stopped supporting me and my efforts. Some physically, many emotionally and a few financially. This is why I suggest that everyone find a way to develop a 'Master Mind Group' that will hold you accountable and applaud your successes and try and help you figure out what went wrong in those other cases.

OTHER RESOURCES

The resources used to create a book like this come from over 30 years in business in almost every possible role. From my Lemonade Stand at age 10 to my Consulting company at age 40, yet I keep returning to the same set of core 'tools' every time I decide to build a long term, sustainable business.

However, I refuse to even try and take credit for myself; instead I'd like to introduce you to some of MY mentors.

I had a young lady; a few years ago tell me for over an hour, how much she wanted to "be just like me." Yet when I referred her to the areas where I gained my abilities, suddenly her career wasn't that important anymore. So please, take my word for it these are some folks you want to "meet" and some books you want to read.

Dale Carnegie: *How to Win Friends and Influence People:*

I knew someone once who *refused* to read this because they were "not interested in controlling other people". After several hours of trying to explain it's actually about getting along with folks, I gave up. Truly one of the greats, if you can find an original copy, get it, the information from the 1930's is just as relevant as today, and a lot more fun to read.

Andy Andrews: *The Noticer:*

I was lucky enough to meet Andy and Polly when he was just getting started in public speaking and before his writing had begun. This was while he was still Americas #1 College Comedian. This book is the beginning of a wonderful exploration of an entire series of discoveries that you may find yourself on, and one that he is well equipped to lead.

Og Mandino: *The Greatest Miracle in the World:*

For years my dad tried to get me to read The Greatest Salesman in the World, and I could just never finish it. However, I finished <u>this</u> book in less than a week and it had a profound impact on my life. I have given many copies of this book away over the years, and in each I make sure to tell folks that if they merely pick it up and start reading it as they would any other they will find that it's a good story. But if you buy it and put it on a shelf until you think that you can't go any farther, than you may discover the miracle. You see the miracle in this book is often discovered only when you feel that 'you' are out of ideas.

Florence Littauer: *Personality Plus*

I knew this was the book that I needed to be reading when I got to the description of my personality and it said "Prefers to make the facts fit the punch line." I encourage everyone to read this book, whether you are a business owner, and employee and investor or somewhere in between, there are few books that I could suggest for you that would have more or better information on the issue of "dealing with people." I have a habit of giving these books away to folks who attend my training sessions, so watch for the next session.

Jerome L. Hess

Other books in this Series:

Remote Control Professional:

The Remote Control term came to me one day, on my way out the door when I realized that I had finally achieved the state of mind with a team that I could relax and know that everything would be "all right" while I was gone. Not a feeling most managers get from their teams. However, anything can be a fluke, so I started to make note of the things that I did that were different from what the other managers were doing. Then at my next management opportunity I started all over again with a new team and new folks and the same tools. They too reached the remote control stage.

Then I started to teach some of my fellow managers some of the techniques that I was using, amazingly enough they received the same results. Science is all about duplicateable results.

Remote Control Manager:

You have just finished Remote Control Professional, in the last 12 chapters you have been exposed to a thumbnail sketch of how I went from Zero to Hero in yet another industry after a life changing injury took me out of Commercial Banking. In Remote Control Management you will find the information that I used to move from a well paid professional employee to a very well paid Manager of People, Teams and millions of dollars in Hardware, Software and Training.

I refuse to say that you must read that book if you hope to reach mangement, but I will tell you that I could not have done so in the relatively short period of time that I did without that information.

Out of Control Networking:

Early on I was introduced to Network Marketing, although back then it was plain old MLM. I learned many lessons along the way to finding my place in the world of business owndersip. Cheif among them is that anytime a mentor offers you 5 minutes, take advantage of all 5 minutes.

Next, when given the opportunity to speak, you do not have to take advantage of it. Additonally you don't have to reinvent the wheel to be successful. If 30 years of folks have come before you and been successful at doing something, what makes you think you have a better idea?

The national Franchisors Association has once again noted that the one career that the most successful Franchise owner comes from, is that of a farmer. Farmers know that they don't know, and they are willing to learn how to do what they want to acheive. After reading *Out of Control Networking* I think that you too will have the toolbox that you need, in order to be completely succesful in whatever it is that you decide to do.

.

www.ingramcontent.com/pod-product-compliance
Lightning Source LLC
Chambersburg PA
CBHW071653200326
41519CB00012BA/2509